VENI VIDI
DIDICI

VENI VIDI DIDICI

Have Fun Learning Latin
with **SONGS, GAMES,
PUZZLES** and **JOKES**

JASON TALLEY

Ulysses Press

Published in the United States by:
Ulysses Press
P.O. Box 3440
Berkeley, CA 94703
www.ulyssespress.com

ISBN: 978-1-61243-673-9
Library of Congress Control Number 2016957555

Printed in Canada by Marquis Book Printing
10 9 8 7 6 5 4 3 2 1

Acquisitions: Casie Vogel
Managing editor: Claire Chun
Editor: David Sweet
Proofreader: Shayna Keyles
Front cover design: Rebecca Lown
Interior design and layout: what!design @ whatweb.com
Cover illustration: © Valentin Ramon

Distributed by Publishers Group West

This book is for my wife, Sarah, who was my nearly constant companion during the research for and writing of this book (though sometimes she was asleep).

This book is also for our children, Stella and Jet, future Latin speakers.

TABLE OF CONTENTS

INTRODUCTION..1

HOW TO USE THIS BOOK......................................3

I. SPEAKING IN TONGUES:
A PRONUNCIATION GUIDE...........................6

ON PRONUNCIATION......................................6

VOWELS..9

DIPHTHONGS...10

CONSONANTS...11

SPECIAL SOUNDS.......................................14

ACCENT...15

MAJOR ECCLESIASTICAL DIFFERENCES......................16

BEFORE YOU MOVE ON...................................18

II. MAKE YOUR OWN LATIN PROVERBS! (AND LEARN
HOW TO USE A LATIN DICTIONARY).................22

VERBS..23

NOUNS..26

III. BEING SOCIAL IN LATIN......................28

GREETING AND LEAVING.................................29

GETTING BY: SURVIVAL PHRASES.........................30

QUESTION BASICS......................................31

GETTING TO KNOW YOU..................................34

MAKING PLANS...39

GOING TO DINNER......................................41

VISITS WITH FRIENDS..................................42

GOING DIGITAL..44

IV. LATIN WITH A BEAT...........................47

BEFORE THE BEAT DROPS................................47

FROM WORDS TO BEATS (SYLLABIFICATION)................50

POETIC FEET 52

ELISION 52

HENDECASYLLABICS 53

DACTYLIC HEXAMETER 57

ELEGAIC COUPLETS 59

METER CHALLENGE 61

V. PLAYING AROUND IN LATIN 64

LŪDĪ RŌMĀNĪ (ROMAN GAMES) 64

TROPĀ 65

MICĀTIŌ 67

ĀLEAE/TESSERAE/TĀLĪ 69

TĀLĪ/ASTROGALOI 70

LATRUNCULĪ 72

XII SCRĪPTŌRUM 75

VI. LATIN SONGS 77

STANDARDS 79

SONGS WRITTEN IN LATIN 83

MODERN LATIN SONGS 91

VII. VULGAR LATIN: THE LATIN OF THE PEOPLE 93

EXAMPLES OF VULGAR LATIN 95

VIII. LATIN JOKES 102

QUINTILIAN 102

CICERO 107

PHILOGELOS 109

IX. KINGS OF LATIN COMEDY 114

PLAUTUS (CA. 254–184 BCE) 115

CATULLUS (CA. 84–54 BCE) 117

HORACE (65–8 BCE) 120

TERENCE (CA. 186/185–CA. 159 BCE) 122

PETRONIUS (CA. 27–66 CE) 124

JUVENAL (CA. 55–CA. 127 CE) 126

MARTIAL (CA. 40–103 CE) 129

APULEIUS (124–170 CE) 132

X. HOW TO ROAST SOMEONE IN LATIN 135

ROASTING 136

PRAISING 140

LAUS PRAISE, COMMENDATION 140

A CAUTIONARY TALE: CICERO'S LAST ROAST 142

ROAST OF JULIUS CAESAR 143

APPENDIX 145

AUTHORS 145

NUMBERS 147

RECOMMENDATIONS FOR FURTHER EXPLORATION 149

ACKNOWLEDGMENTS 155

ABOUT THE AUTHOR 157

INTRODUCTION

The first most common question I get as a Latin teacher is, "Is that like Spanish or something?" The second most common question is, "Isn't that a dead language?" I usually tell people that Hittite and Ancient Egyptian are dead and that Latin is only sleeping; we just need to wake it up. I have heard other teachers describe Latin as a zombie language. The process of teaching Latin has also been referred to more benignly as being like programming a computer. Whatever analogy you care to use, the reports of Latin's death and dullness have been greatly exaggerated.

This little book is for anyone who shares in the belief that Latin is not a dead language, as it has been popularly described. While it is true that native Latin speakers are all dead, their language has continued to exist, grow, and evolve throughout the millennia. Latin was the language of the natural sciences, philosophy, and religion in Europe for centuries, and many American founding fathers were students of Latin. As recently as 100 years ago, Latin translation and even composition played a large part in the entrance exams to Ivy League universities. If Latin is sleeping, it only has been for a few decades of the 20th century. That's hardly a blink in the long history of Latin! The beginning decades of the 21st century have seen an increasingly growing surge of Latin enthusiasts pushing and prodding it to wake up. Tomorrow's Latinist not only will translate and analyze the Latin of the past but will collaborate in creating the Latin of the future. This book is for anyone who wants to be part of writing that future.

As soon as you begin learning any new skill, be it jamming on a didgeridoo, playing badminton, or shouting in Klingon, you start to build a part of your brain that specializes in that skill. Once that part has been created, the only way for it to grow is by exercising it, by practicing. For languages, whether Klingon, Spanish, English, or Latin, you exercise by listening to or reading quality texts that are authentic and comprehensible. Speaking Latin with others can be a great way to get input and get feedback on your speaking or writing skills.

This book gives you the tools you need to exercise and build your Latin brain. Throughout, you will find many different ways to perfect your pronunciation, practice speaking conversationally, and develop an appreciation of Latin literary styles. There are songs to sing, games to play, puzzles to solve, and jokes to tell. There are timeless quotes—some well known, others obscure—from some of the most preeminent Latin writers whose words and works were not completely lost to history, as well as excerpts from satirical and invective poetry written by some of the most scurrilous Roman poets. There are even graffiti and bathroom scribbles, some of the last vestiges of the Vulgar Latin of the streets. There are tidbits on etymology and grammar for language nerds, and interesting facts from Roman history and mythology for the more serious scholar.

This book is for curious students who want to supplement what's taught in their Latin course, for adventurous Latin teachers who want to introduce more speaking into their classrooms, for former students of Latin who are thinking about resuming their studies, and even for people who have never studied Latin before. It is the perfect book for Latin lovers old and new to build their Latin brains.

HOW TO USE THIS BOOK

This book is not meant to be read from *ab malō usque ad ōva* (from beginning to end). If you are a *tīrō* (newcomer) and need to know the basics (or if you are a veteran who needs a refresher), I suggest that you start with the first four chapters, which will orient you to some basic Latin skills: pronunciation, dictionary use, basic conversation, and reading poetry. Otherwise, the reader is invited to hop around to whichever sections are of most interest. I hope that many of the selections and topics will serve as a springboard from which the reader may start a unique journey, exploring all the varieties of work that is accessible with Latin, both ancient and modern.

In Chapter I, you will learn how to pronounce the Latin you will read in this book.

In Chapter II, you will learn how to use a Latin dictionary and make your own versions of famous proverbs.

In Chapter III, you will learn how to talk to other people who know Latin.

In Chapter IV, you will learn about Latin poetry and how to read the poems that appear in this book.

In Chapter V, you will find ancient Roman games to play.

In Chapter VI, you will find songs to sing.

In Chapter VII, you will find Latin graffiti and inscriptions.

In Chapter VIII, you will find jokes to tell.

In Chapter IX, you will find humorous excerpts from ancient authors.

In Chapter X, you will learn how to roast your friends.

In the appendices, there is a page about Latin numbers and a list of the authors mentioned throughout the text.

The capitalization standards have varied across time and texts. I learned that only proper nouns are capitalized, with even the first letter of a sentence left uncapitalized (gasp!) unless it was a proper noun. Some textbooks keep to this standard, some don't. In some Latin poetry texts, you will see capital letters at the beginning of lines. In some texts, modern capitalization standards are followed. Similarly, the Romans did not have punctuation like ours, so punctuation standards of Latin texts have also been varied.

You will see the following sidebars from time to time:

NB

nōtā bene (NB)   note well, mark well

These are the most frequent sidebars, and are used to draw your attention to an important detail you must keep in mind, or just to give a fun fact.

EG

exemplī grātiā (EG)   for the sake of example

These sidebars give examples of some sentence structure mentioned in the text.

GRAMMATICA

grammatica   grammar things

These sidebars will give the reader grammatical forms that are relevant to the section in which they are found.

I

SPEAKING IN TONGUES: A PRONUNCIATION GUIDE

ON PRONUNCIATION

There are two primary ways of pronouncing Latin that are currently taught: Classical and Ecclesiastical Latin.

Classical Latin emerged in the 19th century out of a desire to experience the Latin of Caesar, Cicero, and Catullus as the Romans themselves would have experienced it. Though we don't actually have audio examples of what Latin sounded like from the mouth of a native Latin speaker living at the time of the early Roman Empire, Latinists have been able to figure out the way Latin would have sounded using a variety of methods, including Latin descriptions written by ancient grammarians.

These stuffy fellows not only wrote down instructions and rules for proper pronunciation, but they also complained about the common mispronunciations and spelling errors plaguing their eras. These complaints give us insight into what was considered to be the proper way to speak Latin.

If you go to a Catholic church for Latin Mass or listen to a choir sing Latin songs, you will hear the Ecclesiastical pronunciation. Latin as a semi-living spoken language has been preserved through the millennia by the Roman Catholic Church. It wasn't until the 1960s that the Vatican relaxed the rules requiring Latin Mass. Latin was the official language of the country of Vatican City until Italian replaced it in 2014 (now it is a secondary language, along with French). Even today, through its Latinitas Foundation, the Vatican creates and compiles Latin neologisms (new words) that assist speakers in using Latin successfully in the modern world.

NB

The *American Heritage Dictionary* defines Latinist as a "specialist in Latin." This is like how biologists are scientists who specialize in the study of life and geologists specialize in the study of the earth. It is also given a more general meaning in *Collins English Dictionary* as one who studies Latin. By this definition, you, dear reader, are a budding Latinist and will continue to be a Latinist so long as you continue to try to immerse yourself in Latin by listening to it and reading it.

To sum up, Classical Latin is Latin as it was then, and Ecclesiastical Latin is Latin as it is today.

But in real life, there aren't only two ways of pronouncing Latin. As with English today, the pronunciation of the language varied (sometimes greatly) depending on the region where it was spoken. Over time these variations evolved into separate languages such as Spanish, French, and Romanian. The way that Latin is pronounced today varies in subtle ways, mostly depending on how speakers learned to speak Latin and on the influence from their native language. There are currently two news summaries produced in Latin, both called *Nūntiī Latīnī*—one by the Finnish Yle radio (http://areena.yle.fi/1-1931339) and the other by the German Radio Bremen (http://www.radiobremen .de/nachrichten/latein). If you listen to these two broadcasts, you will hear subtle differences in pronunciation.

I first learned how to pronounce Latin in the Classical fashion and read primarily Classical authors. In recent years, I have trained myself to speak and pronounce in an Ecclesiastical fashion as well. To me, it's similar to switching between different accents in English. Knowing Ecclesiastical pronunciation gives you the ability to read and appreciate Medieval and later Latin "as it was written;" knowing Classical pronunciation gives you the ability to read and appreciate Classical texts.

We will start with a full pronunciation guide for Classical Latin and then show how its pronunciation differs from that of Ecclesiastical Latin. Use this guide as a jumping-off point to discover your own personal way(s) of speaking Latin. Based on your needs, the texts you read, the podcasts you listen to, and the people you converse with in Latin, you will develop your own personal style of speaking the language.

VOWELS

The Latin word for "vowel" is *vōcālis*, from *vōcāre* (to call). A vowel is a sound that can be made on its own. Twelve different sounds are represented by Latin vowels. The long mark, called a macron, is sometimes used to mark the difference between short vowel sounds and long vowel sounds. Macrons are helpful (some say essential) in learning the correct pronunciation and accent of words.

Sometimes changing the vowel length will change the meaning of words in subtle (or not so subtle) ways:

lātrō (**LAH**-troh) I am barking
ā is like the sound you make for the doctor, "Ah!"

latrō (**LA**-troh) robber
a is like the maniacal laugh, "Bwa-ha-ha-ha-ha!"

ēdit (**AY**-dit) he/she/it has eaten
ē is like the sound in Fonzie's famous "Ayyyy!"

edit (**E**-dit) he/she/it is eating
e is like in "Meh!"

līber (**LEE**-ber) child /free
ī is like in "Eek!" and "Whee!"

liber (**LI**-ber) book
i is like in "Ick!"

ōs (**OHS**) mouth
ō is a reactive "Oh!"

os (**OS**) bone
o is like in "Gosh!"

ūter (**OO**-ter) leather bag bottle
ū is an amazed "Ooh!"

uter (**U**-ter) which one?
u is the sound heard in "good" and "put"

NB

The Latin vowel *y* (Greek upsilon) is pronounced like French *u* or German *ü*; this sound is not really heard in English, but it can be found at the end of the word "few" and in the way "syrup" is pronounced by some folks.

There are short and long versions of *y*, but the difference is one of emphasis, not in the represented sound. In contrast to English, *y* is always a vowel in Latin and never a consonant.

DIPHTHONGS

The word "diphthong" comes from the Greek *di* (two) and *phtongos* (vowel). A diphthong is a sound that is represented by two vowels. There are six diphthongs in Latin, related here to familiar English interjections:

ae AYE!
babae! (sounds like ba-b**ye**) woah! (humorously translated as "odds bodkins! wonderful! strange!" in one dictionary, an expression of wonder and joy)

eu E-YOO!
ēheu! (sounds like ay-**heyoo**) oh no! ah! alas! (expression of grief or pain)

au OW!
hau! (sounds like h**ow**) oh! (expression of pain or surprise)

oe OY!

euhoe! (sounds like ayoo-h**oy**) woo-hoo! (a shout of joy at the festivals of Bacchus)

ei EH?

hei (sounds like h**ey**) ah! o dear! (expression of grief or fear)

ui OO-WEE!

hui (sounds like h**oo-wee**) ho! oh! (expression of astonishment or admiration)

CONSONANTS

The word "consonant" comes from the Latin roots *con* (with) and *sonare* (to sound). In Latin and Romance languages, consonants never make a sound on their own, but always make their sound together with a vowel.

būbō	(BOO-bow)	ow
cachinnātiō	(cac-hin-NAH-tyoh) (*c* is always hard)	violent or excessive laughter
dēspiciendus	(day-spi-ci-EN-dus)	contemptible
faciō	(FAH-key-yo)	I do
gemellipara	(geh-mel-LIH-pah-rah) (*g* is always hard)	mother of twins
homunculus	(ho-MUN-cu-lus)	little man

iēiūnitās	(yay-YOU-nih-tahs) (*i* functions as a consonant in front of vowels/dipthongs)	fasting, emptiness of the stomach
kalumniātor	(ka-lum-ni-AH-tor) (*k* is rarely used; *c* is preferred)	a contriver of tricks
longinquitās	(lon-YIN-kwi-tahs)	distance, remoteness, duration
mūculentus	(moo-cu-LEN-tus)	sniveling
nucifrangibulum	(nu-ki-fran-GI-bu-lum)	nutcracker
pedetemptim	(pe-de-TEM-ptim)	step by step, cautiously
quidquid	(QWID-qwid) (*q* always goes with *u*, making the KW sound)	whatever
ructābundus	(ruck-tah-BUN-dus)	belching again and again

somnīculōsus	(som-nee-ku-LO- sus) (always s as in "snake," not "vision")	sleepy, drowsy
turpilucrīcupidus	(tur-pi-lu-cree-CU-pi- dus)	title
vāticinātrix	(wah-ta-ci-NAH-triks) (v always sounds like an English w)	prophetess, fortune-teller
xērampelinae	(ksay-ram-PEL-i-nye)	dark red clothes
zinzilulāre	(zin-zil-ul-ARE-eh)	to chirp

NB

j: There is no letter *j* in Classical Latin; however, Ecclesiastical Latin represents the sound of consonantal *i* with the letter *j* (*jēiūnitās* instead of *iēiūnitās*, with the same pronunciation).

w: There is no letter *w* in Latin; the English sound is represented by the letter *v*.

SPECIAL SOUNDS

Certain combinations of consonants make special sounds that don't appear in English. These can especially be weird when pronouncing words that are ancestors of modern words. For example:

sc is pronounced *sk*, so *scientia* (science) is pronounced ski-EN-ti-a.

bs is pronounced *ps*, like the Greek letter *psi*, so *urbs* (from which we get the English words "urban" and "suburban") is pronounced urps.

bt is pronounced *pt*, so *obtrectātiō* (disparagement, detraction) is pronounced op-trec-TAH-tyoh.

gn is pronounced *ngn* like in the English term "wing nut," so *magnus* (big, great) is pronounced mang-nus.

gu/ngu is pronounced *gw* like in the English name Gwen, so *sanguis* (blood) is pronounced san-gwis.

ph is an "aspirated" *p*, which is a *p* plus a breath (*h*) (represented in Greek by the letter *phi*). You can feel the difference between an unaspirated *p* and an aspirated *p* if you hold your hand in front of your mouth while saying the English words "up" and "uphill." Thus *philosophia* sounds more like pill-ow-sop-PY-a than the way we pronounce "philosophy" in English.

th is an "aspirated" *t*, which is a *t* plus a breath (*h*) (represented in Greek by the letter *theta*). You can feel the difference between an unaspirated *t* and aspirated *t* if you hold your hand in front of your mouth while saying the English words "ant" and "anthill." Thus *theātrum* sounds more like t(h)e-AHT-rum than the way we pronounce "theater" in English.

ch is pronounced like the *ch* in the English word "ache." Thus the monster/whirlpool Charybdis from Greek mythology is pronounced c(h)a-RIB-dis like "chorus," not "chair."

ACCENT

Accent has to do with which syl-LAB-les the em-PHA-sis is placed on within a word, and is capitalized in this book. A Latin word has as many syllables as it has vowels and diphthongs.

In multisyllabic words, the accent falls on either the penult (next to last syllable) or the antepenult (before the next to last syllable). The accent never falls on the last syllable.

it (IT) he/she/it goes
facit (FA-cit) he/she/it makes/does
accidit (AC-ci-dit) it happens

To find out where the accent falls, you need to look at the vowels within a word.

If the next to last vowel is long by nature or long by position (immediately followed by two or more consonants), the accent will fall on this syllable (penult).

effēcit (ef-FAY-cit) he/she/it accomplished
discessērunt (di-skes-SAY-runt) they left
nōmen (NOH-men) name

If the next to last vowel is short (i.e., not long), the accent will fall on the preceding syllable (antepenult).

efficit (EF-fi-cit) he/she/it accomplishes
discesserant (dis-SKES-er-ant) they had left
nōmina (NOH-mi-na) names

MAJOR ECCLESIASTICAL DIFFERENCES

Vowels and diphthongs are pronounced more or less the same in both Ecclesiastical and Classical Latin. Several different online sources present differing "rules" on how vowels should (and shouldn't) be pronounced ecclesiastically. I have seen some rules for vowels that follow the Classical rules (except for diphthongs), with a long and short version of each vowel. Many others prescribe the use of only one sound for each vowel, with the difference between long and short being the length of the sound rather than a distinct sound. I find that the pronunciation of vowels and diphthongs by some speakers, of both Classical and Ecclesiastical Latin, can be influenced by how the letters are pronounced in the speakers' native language, producing more varieties of spoken Latin. Essentially, it's not a big deal if your vowels don't follow these "rules."

A major difference is the pronunciation of the diphthongs *ae* and *oe*, which are pronounced like *ē*; thus *caelum* (sky) is chay-lum, not caye-lum. Also, *ē* is not pronounced as "ay" in Ecclesiastical Latin.

Other major differences are in the sounds of consonants, some of which change according to the vowels they are interacting with:

ECCLESIASTICAL PRONUNCIATION RULE	ECCLESIASTICAL EXAMPLE	CLASSICAL EXAMPLE
c is pronounced like *ch* in "chin" before *e*, *i*, *ae*, and *oe*	*celer* (quick) is CHE-ler	*celer* (quick) is KE-ler
g is soft (pronounced like a *j*) when it comes before *e* or *i*	*genius* (spirit) is JEN-yus	*genius* (spirit) is GEN-yus, with a hard *g*
j is sometimes used to represent the consonantal *i*	*jānua* (door) is also YA-nu-a	*iānua* (door) is YA-nu-a
s is pronounced *z*: - when between two vowels - following a consonant at the end of a word	*miseria* (misery) is mi-ZER-ya *fors* (fate) is FORZ	*miseria* (misery) is mi-SER-ya *fors* (fate) is FORS with a hard *s*
v is pronounced like the English *v*; this is one of the major differences between the two modes of pronouncing Latin	Caesar's *vēnī, vīdī, vīcī* is VE-nee, VE-dee, WE-chee	Caesar's *vēnī, vīdī, vīcī* is WAY-nee, WE-dee, WE-key
x is pronounced *gz* when followed by a vowel, *h*, or *s*	*existō* (I exist) is egz-IS-toh	*existō* (I exist) is ex-IS-toh

Some consonant combinations are different as well:

ECCLESIASTICAL PRONUNCIATION RULE	ECCLESIASTICAL EXAMPLE	CLASSICAL EXAMPLE
cc is pronounced like *ch* in "chin" before the letters *e* and *i*	*accidit* (it happens) is a-CHI-dit	*accidit* (it happens) is ak-KI-dit
gg is pronounced like *j* in "edge" before the letters *e* and *I*	*agger* (a pile) is A-jer	*agger* (a pile) is AG-ger
gn is pronounced like *ny* in the English taunt "nyah-nyah"	*magnus* (big, great) is MAN-yus	*magnus* (big, great) is MANG-nus
sc is pronounced like *sh* in "shut" before the letters *e* and *i*	*nesciō* ("I don't know") is NE-shi-o	*nesciō* (I don't know) is NE-ski-o
ti is pronounced *tzy* like in "ditzy" when it comes between two vowels	*ratiō* (reason) is RA-tzi-o	*ratiō* (reason) is RA-ti-o
bs is pronounced *bz*	*urbs* (city) is URBZ	*urbs* (city) is URPS
bt is pronounced as written	*obtrectātiō* is ob-trec-TA-ti-o	*obtrectātiō* is op-trec-TA-ti-o
ph is pronounced *f*	*philosophia* is fi-lo-SO-fi-a	*philosophia* is pi-lo-SO-pi-a
ch/th are pronounced more like *c* and *t*, without the aspirates	*theātrum* is te-AT-rum Charybdis is ca-RYB-dis	*theātrum* is t(h)e-AT-rum Charybdis is c(h)a-RYB-dis

BEFORE YOU MOVE ON

Perfecting proper pronunciation requires patience and persistent practice. This chapter presents a jumping-off point for a lifetime of enjoyment of Latin as Latin. To fully understand, enjoy, and appreciate the Latin you read, you should always try to read it aloud so that you can develop a taste for the words. The sentences presented below offer a tongue-twisting speed challenge, but in truth, the entire book is full of examples that you can chew on as you begin to digest and absorb the language.

LATIN PRONUNCIATION CHALLENGE

Try to pronounce the following sentences as quickly as you can. Some of these are also examples of verses explained in Chapter IV. (Bonus: Can you find the sentence that is a palindrome?)

1. avē, ave, aveō ēsse avēs.
   Hail, grandfather, I want to eat birds.

2. vērus amīcus noscitur ex amōre mōre ōre rē.
   A true friend is known by their love,
   behavior, mouth, reality [literally, his or her thing].

3. persevērā, per sevēra, per sē vēra.
   Persevere through the harsh things, which are true in themselves.

4. ō Tite tūte Tatī tibi tanta tyranne tulistī!
   O Titus Tatius, safe one, you tyrant, you brought such great things for yourself!
   [This fragment from the ancient poet Ennius is also a complete line of poetry. See Chapter IV.]

5. in marī merī mīrī morī mūrī necesse est.
   In a sea of pure honey wine, the mouse has got to die.

6. est bellum bellīs bellum bellāre puellīs.
   It is good to wage war for pretty girls.

7. tē terō, Rōma, manū nūdā, dāte tēla, latēte!

I will rub you away, Rome, with my bare hand, give your weapons, hide!

8. mālō mālō malō mālō.

I'd rather be in an apple tree than be a bad man on a mast.

9. in gȳrum īmus nocte et consūmimur ignī.

We go into the circle by night and are consumed by the fire.

10. perturbābantur Constantīnopolītānī innumerābilibus sollicitūdinibus.

The Constantinopolites were disturbed by countless worries.

11. cāne dēcane, canis: sed nē cane, cāne dēcane, dē cane; dē cānīs, cāne dēcane, cane.

Gray-haired dean, you sing, but don't sing, gray-haired dean, about your dog;
about your gray hairs, gray-haired dean, sing.

12. mīmī nūminum nivium minimī mūnium nimium vīnī mūnīminum imminuī vīvī minimum volunt.

The smallest living mimes of the snow divinities minimally want the defense of too ready wine to be lightened while they are living.

[This Latin tongue twister is not only gobbledygook in English, but is really difficult to read if you see it in medieval script.]

LATIN PRONUNCIATION
CHALLENGE ANSWERS

1. A-way, A-weh, A-we-oh AYS-se A-ways.

2. WAY-rus ah-MEE-cus NOS-ci-tur EX a-MOH-re MOH-re OH-re RAY.

3. perse-WAY-rah, PER se-VAY-ra, PER SAY VAY-ra.

4. OH TI-te TOO-te TA-tee TI-bi TAN-ta tuh-RAN-ne tu-LIS-tee!

5. IN MA-ree ME-ree MEE-ree MO-ree MOO-ree ne-CES-se EST.

6. EST BEL-lum BEL-lees BEL-lum bel-LAH-re pu-EL-lees.

7. TAY TE-roh, ROH-ma, MA-noo NOO-dah, DAH-te TAY-la, la-TAY-te!

8. MAH-loh MAH-loh MA-loh MAH-loh.

9. IN GUH-rum EE-mus NOC-te ET con-SOO-mi-mur IG-nee (This one is the palindrome).

10. per-tur-bah-BAN-tur con-stan-tee-no-po-lee-TAH-nee in-nu-me-rah-BI-li-bus sol-li-ci-too-DI-ni-bus.

11. CAH-ne DAY-ca-ne, CA-nis: SED NAY CA-ne, CAH-ne DAY-ca-ne, DAY CA-ne; DAY CAH-neess, CAH-ne DAY-ca-ne, CA-ne.

12. MEE-mee NOO-mi-num NI-wi-um MI-ni-mee MOO-ni-um NI-mi-um VEE-nee moo-NEE-mi-num im-MI-nu-ee WEE-wee MI-ni-mum VO-lunt.

II

MAKE YOUR OWN LATIN PROVERBS! (AND LEARN HOW TO USE A LATIN DICTIONARY)

Before we begin this chapter on dictionary skills, please consider this brief public service announcement:

Are you unable to understand what you read in Latin without constantly looking up each and every word? Do you constantly flip through the dictionary, frustrated and unable to find the word you need? Is reading Latin—dare I say—a boring task for you? If so, you may suffer from dictionary addiction.

I once suffered from dictionary addiction. When approaching a Latin text, I had to have a dictionary, sometimes even a lexicon, a grammar reference, and something to write all my notes on; sometimes I even needed an English translation. Thanks to being able to use Latin actively, I have weaned myself off my need for dictionaries and reference materials. Now I can read a Latin text on its own, as I do with English texts. I still use the dictionary from time to time for reference, but not nearly as much as I used to, and not for understanding what happens in a sentence or passage.

Curing dictionary addiction is beyond the scope of this book, but it is a scourge that must be identified and guarded against. But regardless of its dangers, using a dictionary is a special skill that every Latinist must develop in order to be successful. It's easy enough if you want to look up conjunctions, adverbs, participles, or interjections. But try to look up a specific form of a noun, pronoun, adjective, or verb and you won't find it. The listings in Latin dictionaries are written in a particular way. Once you know how to use it, the secrets of the Latin dictionary will give you much power, for when you have the dictionary form of a noun or verb, you can build any possible form of that word. Just remember to guard yourself against dictionary addiction.

VERBS

Most verbs are presented in a dictionary with four principal parts: the present (I verb), the infinitive (to verb), the perfect (I have verbed), and the perfect passive participle (having been verbed). Use the following activity to get accustomed to these four principal parts of Latin verbs and create some silly versions of famous Latin proverbs.

The classic example is *amō, amāre, amāvī, amātus*:

amō   I love (first principal part)

amāre   to love (second principal part)

amāvī   I loved (third principal part)

amātus   having been loved (fourth principal part)

NB

If you are looking up a word in an English-Latin dictionary, you will see only the first principal part (sometimes the second). Make sure to cross-reference the word in a Latin-English dictionary to see the other principal parts and get a fuller idea of the word's meaning(s).

Looking up "love" will yield *colō* and *dīligō*, in addition to *amō*. If you then look in the Latin-English dictionary you will find that the full forms of these verbs are:

amō, amāre, amāvī, amātus   to love, be fond of

colō, colere, coluī, cultus   to till, cultivate, cherish, honor, worship, love

dīligō, dīligere, dīlexī, dīlectus   to value, esteem, love

Pick a random verb from the Latin dictionary or find the Latin equivalent of an English word. Once you've chosen your word, replace the underlined word in each of the following proverbs with the appropriate principal part of your verb and impress your friends with your new Latin creation:

First Principal Part: Present Active, "I Verb/I Am Verbing"

cogitō ergo sum. —Descartes
I think therefore I am.

_____ *ergo sum.*

Second Principal Part: Infinitive, "To Verb"

errāre hūmānum est. —Seneca
To err is human.

_____ *hūmānum est.*

Third Principal Part: Perfect, "I (Have) Verbed"

vēnī, vīdī, vīcī. —Caesar
I came, I saw, I conquered.

vēnī, vīdī, _____.

Fourth Principal Part: Perfect Passive Participle, "(Having Been) Verbed"

alea iacta est. —Caesar
The die is cast.

alea _____ *est.* (Change the *-us* form in the dictionary to *-a*.)

GRAMMATICA

Different endings are required for nouns. Masculine nouns get an -us ending, feminine nouns get an -a ending, and neuter nouns get an -um ending.

NB

"Case" refers to different forms of nouns based on their use in a sentence. Latin's five main cases are usually presented in this order: nominative, genitive, dative, accusative, and ablative.

NOUNS

There are many different forms of Latin nouns, depending on how the noun functions in a sentence. These different forms are called cases. The chart below explains the function of each case and shows an example in Latin.

CASE NAME	FUNCTION	LATIN EXAMPLE	ENGLISH TRANSLATION
Nominative	subject of a verb	**puella** nautam amat.	**The girl** loves the sailor.
Genitive	possessive form of the noun	nauta felem **puellae** amat.	The sailor loves **the girl's** cat.
Dative	indirect object of a verb	nauta **puellae** rosam dat.	The sailor gives a rose **to the girl**.
Accusative	direct object of a verb	nauta **puellam** amat.	The sailor loves **the girl**.
Ablative	used in various prepositional and adverbial phrases	nauta cum **puellā** ambulat.	The sailor walks with **the girl**.

When you look up a noun in a Latin dictionary, you will only see two cases: the nominative and the genitive.

EG

The word for "love" is listed in the dictionary as *amor, amōris*:

amor   a/the love (nominative subject)

amōris   of a/the love, a/the love's (genitive possessive)

Below are two proverbs whose nouns you can fill in.

Nominative: A/The Noun

amor omnia vincit. —Ovid
Love conquers all.

_____ *omnia vincit.*

Genitive: Noun's/Of the Noun

ars gratiā artis —MGM motto
Art for the sake of art

ars gratiā _____

EG

placenta, -ae   cake

placenta omnia vincit   Cake conquers all.

ars gratiā placentae   Art for the sake of cake.

III

BEING SOCIAL
IN LATIN

You might think that, barring being trapped in a time warp and finding yourself in ancient Rome, all of your interactions with other Latin speakers will be in a classroom. But the fun doesn't have to stop in the ivory tower. Believe it or not, you can find a ton of awesome, fun places full of Latin speakers (sometimes small places, but places nonetheless). Groups across the world meet for meals and speak Latin, and even summer camps are conducted in Latin (also available during other seasons). If you can't find people to meet up with locally, you can check out groups of Latin speakers online (there's even a World of Warcraft clan).

The goal of this chapter is to get you started speaking Latin actively and help you confidently navigate whatever spoken Latin community you choose to explore. Remember that listening to others speak Latin will be a great way for you to exercise your Latin brain. Make sure to ask others the kinds of questions that will either be understandable to you or help you advance your knowledge of the vocabulary and grammar of Latin. Listen actively to their answers, and most of all, have fun and rejoice in the fact that you are speaking to a fellow human in a language that is more than 2,000 years old. By the end of this chapter, you'll be able to say hello, make new friends, order a meal, and even have some virtual adventures—in Latin! This section also gives basic information about Latin grammar with practical applications. The grammatical information presented here is the most basic. If you are interested in further explanation of Latin grammar, see the resources listed at the end of the book.

GREETING AND LEAVING

One of the first things to realize about some Latin words is that they change their forms depending on their meaning. For example, different forms of verbs depend on the "number" of subjects associated with the action indicated.

salvē!	Hello! (to one person)
salvēte!	Hello! (to two or more people)
avē! hail!	Hello! (to one person)
avēte! hail!	Hello! (to two or more people)
bonum mātūtīnum!	Good morning!
bonum diem!	Good day!
bonum vesperum!	Good evening!
quid agis?	How are you doing?/What's up?

NB

quid agis? can also mean "what are you doing?," but I use *quid facis?* for that question.

It can be abbreviated as *qu'agis?*

optimē!	Very well!
bene!	Well!
variē!	So-so!
male!	Badly!
pessimē!	Very badly!
valē!/valēte!	Goodbye!
bonum noctem!	Good night!
habē/habēte bonum diem/ bonam noctem/bonum biduum!	Have a good day/good night/ good weekend!

GETTING BY: SURVIVAL PHRASES

The following phrases are necessary for successfully navigating any community of Latin speakers in which you might find yourself:

ita	Yes	minimē	No
nēsciō	I don't know	repete	Repeat
dīc iterum	Say it again	dīc lentius	Say it slower

manifestum nōn est	It is not clear	nōn intellegō	I do not understand
quaesō	Please	libenter	You're welcome. (gladly)
grātiās (tibi agō)	Thank you		

Here are things to say to make it seem like you're listening:

babae!	Woah!	mactē!	Well done!
mīrābile!	Miraculous!	dī immortālēs!	Immortal gods!
ain'?	You don't say?	vērē?	Really?
euge!	Woo!	ēheu!	Oh no!

QUESTION BASICS

There are three possible ways to ask a yes or no question:

1. **ne**   Yes/no question
   esne īrāta?   (Are you angry?)

2. **nōnne?**   Surely? (expects a yes answer)
   nōnne īrāta es?   (Aren't you angry?)

3. **num?**   Surely not? (expects a no answer)
   num īrāta es?   (You aren't angry, are you?)

Questions can also be formed by using interrogative pronouns. Many interrogatives are used in Latin. Presented here are the basic 5Ws and H:

quis	Who?
quis es? ___ sum.	Who are you? I am ___.
quis sum? tū es ___.	Who am I? You are ___.
quis est? Is/ea est ___.	Who is it? He/She is ___.
quī sunt? eī/eae sunt ___.	Who are they? They(m)/they(f) are ___.

NB

Pronouns stand in for nouns. The first and second person pronouns are easy enough:

ego	I	**tū**	you
nōs	we	**vōs**	you all

Things get more complicated when talking in the third person. This is because Latin nouns have three "genders." The first two genders are masculine and feminine. It is important to note that gender is a grammatical concept and does not have to do with the biological sex of the noun indicated (if any):

is	he	**ea**	she

eī/iī they (group made partly or wholly of masculine nouns)

eae they (group made wholly of feminine nouns)

Each of these pronoun forms has separate case forms (different forms for different usages in sentences) that must be learned.

Unlike most modern Romance languages, there is no distinction of formality in forms of the pronouns in Latin. You are more likely to see a writer using the royal "we" to refer to themselves!

quid	What?
quid est? id est ___.	What is it? It is ___.
quae sunt? eae sunt ___.	What are they? They are ___.

NB

Neuter nouns make up the third gender of Latin nouns. They are neither masculine nor feminine. Here are the third person neuter pronouns:

id   it

ea   they (group made wholly of neuter nouns)

ubi?	Where?
ubi est? id est in ___.	Where is it? It is in ___.
quandō?	When?
quandō est? nuncinunc est.	When is it? It is right now.
cūr?	Why?
cūr est? quia est.	Why is it? Because it is.
quōmodo?	How?
quōmodo est? satis est.	How is it? It is OK.

Latin verbs also change according to the person or subject performing the action indicated by the verb.

The following endings are present tense personal endings:

nēsciō	I don't know	nēscīmus	**We** don't know
nēscīs	**You** do not understand	nēscītis	**You all** don't know
nēscit	**He/She/It** does not understand	nēsciunt	**They** don't know

GETTING TO KNOW YOU

quis es?	Who are you?
___ sum.	I am ___.
quid est nōmen tibi?	What is the name for you?
nōmen mihi est ___.	The name for me is ___.
quid appellāris?	What are you named?
appellor ___.	I am named ___.

GRAMMATICA

Latin verbs also change according to the relationship of the subject to the verb. This is known as "voice." There are two voices in Latin: active and passive.

When active voice is used, the subject performs the action indicated by the verb. When passive voice is used, the subject receives the action indicated by the verb. Thus, *appellō* (I call, I name) is active and *appellor* (I am called, I am named) is passive.

The endings in the Grammatica box on page 34 are the present tense active verbs. The following endings are the present tense passive endings. Another type of verb, known as a deponent verb, looks passive but is translated actively, and uses these endings:

appellor	I am called	**appellāmur**	**We** are called
appellāris	**You** are called	**appellāminī**	**You all** are called
appellātur	**He/She/It** is called	**appellantur**	**They** are called

quaestio

quot annōs habēs? How many years do you have? How old are you?

___ annōs habeō.	I have ___ years. I am ___ years old.

trīgintā annōs habeō. | I am 30 years old.

quaestio
unde venīs? | From where do you come?

respōnsum
dē ___ veniō. | I come from ___.

dē Austinopole, Texiā veniō. | I come from Austin, Texas.

quaestio
quid per ōtium facis? | What do you do during your leisure time?

quid per negōtium facis? | What do you do during your non-leisure time (work)?

respōnsum
per ōtium ___.
[You can fill this in with any principal part of a verb; see Chapter II: Verbs for some ideas]. | During my free time ___.

per ōtium librōs Latinōs legō. | During my free time I read Latin books.

per ōtium videōludōs lūdō. | During my free time I play video games.

quaestio

quid est liber dīlectus tuus? | What is your favorite book?

respōnsum

liber dīlectus meus est ___ difficile. | My favorite book is ___.

difficile est/legere ōdī. | That's hard/I hate reading.

quaestio

quās fabulās spectās? | What shows do you watch?

respōnsum

___ spectō. | I watch ___.

quaestio

quam musicam audīs? | What music do you listen to?

respōnsum

___ audiō. | I listen to ___.

quaestio

habēsne amīcum/amīcam? | Do you have a boyfriend/girlfriend?

respōnsum

sīc/minimē/nōnne cognoscere velīs? | Yes/no/Wouldn't you like to know?

CATCHING UP

To ask what someone's been up to recently, use *quid fecisti?* (What have you been doing?).

You can also ask the same question more specifically and indicate various times:

quid fēcistī...	What did you do...
nocte peractō?	last night?
per biduum?	over the weekend?
per fēriās?	over the break?
per IV annōs peractōs?	during the last four years?

Your response will be the third principal part of your chosen verb: I verbed.

GRAMMATICA

In addition to person and number, verbs have tenses, which indicate when the action of the verb took place. There are several past tense verb forms in Latin. Responses to the question "What did you do last night?" would give an example of the "perfect" tense, which represents an action completed in the past. These are the perfect personal endings:

fēcī	I did, I have done	**fēcīmus**	**We** did, **We** have done
fēcistī	**You** did, **You** have done	**fēcistis**	**You all** did, **You all** have done
fēcit	**He/She/It** did, **He/She/It** has done	**fēcērunt**	**They** did, **They** have done

The following questions might be handy at your Latin Club Reunion:

quid novī apud tē?	What's new with you?
etiam in Los Angeles habitas?	Do you still live in LA?
habēsne līberos?	Do you have any kids?
etiam colloqueris cum ___?	Do you still talk with ___?
meministīne ___?	Do you remember ___?
umquam ad Taiwan ivistī?	Did you ever go to Taiwan?

MAKING PLANS

quid faciēs...	What are you going to do...
hāc nocte?	tonight?
hōc biduō?	this weekend?
Iovis proximō?	next Thursday?
sēdecimō Iuniī?	on June 16?

Your response will be the future form of your chosen verb: "I will verb."

You could also use *velīsne* (would you want/would you like) plus an infinitive or infinitive phrase to ask about possible plans for the future:

velīsne...	Would you want...
morārī post scholam?	to hang out after school?
īre ad cenam?	to go to dinner?
convenīre amīcōs meōs?	to meet my friends?
mē cum pensō domesticō adiuvāre?	to help me with my homework?
canem meum lavāre?	to wash my dog?

velīsne...	Would you want...
spectāre Netflix apud me?	to watch Netflix at my house?
venīre mēcum in itinere?	to come with me on a trip?
Latīne colloquī?	to talk in Latin?

GRAMMATICA

FUTURE TENSE

There are two ways to form the future tense in Latin:

1. Verbs with *a* and *e* in their infinitive use the following endings: *-bō, -bis, -bit, -bimus, -bitis, -bunt.*

You remove the *-re* from the infinitive and replace it with the ending:

spectāre   *spectā*   *spectābō*

quid hāc nocte faciēs?	What are you going to do tonight?
televisiōnem spectābō.	I am going to watch TV.

2. Verbs with an *e* and *i* in their infinitive use the following endings: *-am, -ēs, -et, -ēmus, -ētis, -ent.*

You remove the *-ere* or *-ire* from the infinitive and replace it with the ending:

lūdere   *lud*   *lūdam*

quid hāc nocte faciēs?	What are you going to do tonight?
videōlūdos lūdam.	I am going to play video games.

GOING TO DINNER

quid edere vīs?	What do you want to eat?
___ volō.	I want ___.
quid bibis/edis?	What are you drinking/eating?
___ bibō/edō.	I'm drinking/eating ___.
umquam hūc cēnāvistī?	Have you ever dined here?
semper/aliquandō hūc cēnō.	I always dine here/I dine here sometimes.
aliquand numquam hūc cēnāvī.	I've never dined here.
ēsuriō!/sitiō!	I'm hungry!/I'm thirsty!
ubi est linteum meum?	Where is my napkin?
estne illa aqua mea an tua?	Is that my water or your water?
trādas illud, quaesō!	Pass that, please!
nesciō quid velim.	I don't know what I want.
habeō quod habeat.	I'm having what she's having.
quid dē cibō pūtās?	What do you think about the food?
hic cibus est sapidus/foedus!	The food is tasty/gross!
minister/ministra! fer chartulam, quaesō!	Waiter/Waitress, bring the check, please!
quot prō praemiō dēmus?	How much should we give for the tip (for the reward)?

This gem from Catullus 13 is perhaps worth remembering when the bill finally shows up:

ēheu! plēnus sacculus est arāneārum!	Oh no! My wallet is full of cobwebs!

VISITS WITH FRIENDS

xenia was an idea of hospitality that existed in the ancient world. It was based on the belief that since the gods could take human form at their will, anyone you encounter could potentially be a god in disguise. *xenia* is the application of this idea to inviting guests into your home. If you are a host, you must remember to treat your guests with the highest respect. If you are ever a guest, you should behave in a way that deserves such great honor and respect. The importance of this guest-host relationship can be seen in the fact that the words *hospēs* and *hospitis* (whence the terms "hospitality" and "hospital") can mean either "guest" or "host," depending on the context.

The following phrases and questions would be useful when visiting the Latin-speaking friends you've made in the far-flung forums of the world.

For talking with others about your trip to wherever you went:

quōmodō erat iter tuum?	How was your trip?
(iter erat) bonum/malum/ longum/taediōsum.	(The trip was) good/bad/long/ boring.
quō modō vēnistī?	How did you come?

autoraedā/āeroplanō/ trāmine/equō/nāve vēnī.	By car/by plane/by train/by horse/by boat I came.
quamdiu erat iter tuum?	How long was your trip?
erat ferē ___ horās.	It was about ___ hours.
vīdistīne aliquid notae in itinere?	Did you see anything of note on the trip?
___ vīsī./nihil notae vīsī.	I saw ___./I saw nothing of note.
convēnistīne aliquem notae in viā?	Did you meet anyone of note on the way?
convēnī ___./nēminem notae convenī.	I met ___./I met no one of note.

For talking about your plans at your destination:

quamdiu apud nōs manēbis?	How long will you be staying with us?
___ horās/diēs/hebdomadēs manēbō.	I will be staying ___ hours/days/weeks.
ubi rēs mihi dēpōnendae sunt?	Where should I put my things?
quae sunt agenda nōbīs?	What are we going to do?
suntne aliquae tabernae bonae in vīcīniā?	Are there any good shops in the area?

And for when you find that things have gone way too late into the night:

fessus/fessa sum! dormiendum mihi est!	I'm tired! I've got to go to sleep!

GOING DIGITAL

You can find Latin communities on Twitter, or Pipatio in Latin, and on games like World of Warcraft and Minecraft. Here are some words and phrases relevant to the digital age:

telephonum callidum	smart phone
tabula (electronica)	tablet (electronic)
computātrum/ordinātrum	computer
interrēte	Internet
tēla	web
inīre/exīre	to log-in/log-off
programma	app/program
media sociābilia	social media
tēlam nāvigāre	to navigate/surf the web
epistulam electronicam mittere	to send an e-mail
pīpiāre	to tweet
videōlūdōs lūdere	to play video games

Here are some questions to try out that will help you flex your Latin brain in the digital world:

quāle telephonum habēs?	What kind of phone do you have?
quot programmās in telephonō habēs? quās?	How many apps do you have on your phone? Which ones?
quī sitūs in tēlā sunt dīlectī tibi?	What sites on the web are your favorite?
quae nuntia in tēlae legis?	What news sites on the web do you read?
habēsne ordinātrum tuum?	Do you have your own computer?
lūdisne videōlūdōs? quōs lūdis?	Do you play video games? Which ones do you play?
quī videolūdī sunt dīlectī?	Which video games are your favorite?
lūdisne in telephonō/ordinātrō/Xbox/PlayStation?	Do you play on your telephone/computer/Xbox/PlayStation?
habēsne pinnam prō iPhone/Android?	Do you have a charger (plug) for an iPhone/Android?
quibus mediīs sociābilibus ūteris?	Which social media (platforms) do you use?

LATIN TEXT-MESSAGE CHALLENGE

Match the message on the right with the correct response on the left.

1. quid velīs spectāre in theātrō?

2. quid fēcistī nocte perāctō?

3. etiam in Novā Aurēliā habitās?

4. quid dē cibō meō putāvistī?

5. quōmodo ad vīllam meam venīs?

6. quam fessa sum! multum nocte perāctō studēbam.

7. quid est nōmen frātris tuī? oblītus sum!

8. quid per fēriās faciēs? vīsne morārī?

9. quam mūsicam audīs?

10. quandō iterum tēcum colloquī poterim?

a. nōn possum! ad Flōridam ībō!

b. cibus tuus erat sapidus! Grātiās!

c. nōn certus sum. fortasse diē Saturnae.

d. novam peliculam "Bellum Stēllārum" spectāre velim.

e. nōmen eius est Mārcus. cūr rogās?

f. nūllam mūsicam, sedpoemās Latīnās audiō!

g. dormiendum tibi est! ī dormītum!

h. ibi equō veniō. habēsne stabulum?

i. minimē, in Novō Eborācō habitō.

j. nōn multum dormīvī, videoludōs lūdēbam.

ANSWERS

1. d   2. j   3. i   4. b   5. h   6. g   7. e   8. a   9. f   10. c

IV

LATIN WITH A BEAT

BEFORE THE BEAT DROPS

Rap is the current art form that is closest to Classical Latin and Ancient Greek poetry. Both art forms focus on delivering words and ideas rhythmically. In them there is much less emphasis on rhyme than in traditional English poetry; instead, other types of wordplay, such as alliteration, allusion, and assonance, are preferred. In addition, some of the writing and thinking processes described by rappers like Eminem, Talib Kweli, Ice-T, and others are identical to those employed by the performing poets of Greece and Rome.

Poetry was the pinnacle of personal success as a writer. Poetry was also an important part of theatrical performances, the other main public form of Latin. A play like *Hamilton* (without the music) would not be foreign to the Roman stage. Topics found in Latin poetry range from tales of epic heroes to astrological and meteorological information, from philosophy to mythology to history. Although many examples of Latin poetry appear throughout the book, this chapter is mainly concerned with scansion.

NB

alliteration: repetition of consonant sounds throughout a line of poetry

allusion: indirect reference of cultural or symbolic significance

assonance: repetition of vowel sounds throughout a line of poetry

Scansion (from *scandere,* to climb) is the process of marking up the long and short syllables in a line of Latin verse and "mapping out" the way the lines of poetry should be read. Depending on your personal learning preferences, it can be really fun or really tedious and boring. Learning how to scan poetry, and thus read it aloud correctly, will allow you a greater appreciation of the Latin poetry, which, again, was written to be read aloud, not translated into English.

The major difference between Latin poetry and English poetry is that Latin poetry is written in a quantitative metrical system, in which emphasis is placed on the syllable length. Here the long marks are equivalent to quarter notes and the short marks are equivalent to eighth notes. English scansion is more concerned with syllable; the long marks represent accented syllables, the short marks unaccented syllables. Note that short syllables are marked "ˇ" and long syllables are marked "—."

Here are two lines from Shakespeare's *Romeo and Juliet*, written in qualitative iambic pentameter:

Yĕa NOĪSE? thĕn I'LL bĕ BRĪEF. ŏ HĀPpў DĀGgĕr

thĭs ĪS thў SHĒATH; thĕre RŪST ănd LĒT mĕ DĪE.

And here are two lines from Ovid's *Metamorphoses*, written in quantitative dactylic hexameter:

SĪGna TĒnĕ CAEdĭs pulLŌSqŭ(ĕ) ĒT LŪCtĭbŭs ĀPtŏs.

SEMpĕr HAbĕ FĒtŭs, GEmĭnī mŏnĭMENta crŭŌrĭs.

As you can see in the Shakespeare example, the long marks always represent a stressed syllable and the short marks always represent an unstressed syllable. In most scansion of Shakespeare, only the stressed syllables are marked, usually with a u or a '.

In the Ovid example, the long and short marks do not correspond to the stress of the words, because they are indicating different vowel lengths.

Though Latin poets used many different meters, the three presented here will give you the ability to access a large amount of Latin poetry. To get the full effect, you should use the Classical pronunciation for the examples presented. Rhythm has a powerful effect on your memory. You can strengthen your Latin brain by memorizing these verses and chanting or singing them, even recording them to listen to later (which will also strengthen your Latin brain). You can also use the meters as a way to organize your own notes or other information to assist with recall and retention.

Challenge 1: Memorize these verses. Once you've mastered all these, start memorizing chunks of other Latin poetry and see how many lines you can store in your head.

Challenge 2: Record yourself reciting these (or other) Latin verses, preferably with instrumental accompaniment and tweet with #LatinWithABeat.

FROM WORDS TO BEATS (SYLLABIFICATION)

Before we look at specific meters, we should pause for a quick refresher about syllabification and poetic meter.

In Latin words, the accent falls on either the penult:

leviōsa   le-we-O-sa

or the antepenult:

vingārdium   win-GAR-di-um

The way you can tell is to look at the next to last syllable. If the penultimate syllable is long by nature or long by position, it will be accented. If not, the antepenultimate syllable will be accented. The concept of long by nature/long by position also comes up in poetry. A vowel is long by nature if it is a naturally long vowel (marked with a macron in many texts) or a diphthong. A vowel is long by position if it is followed by two or more consonants.

The letter *x* by itself counts as two consonants when following a vowel (*ks*).

Sometimes a vowel can be short when followed by two consonants if one of those consonants is *r* or *l*.

If a vowel is neither long by nature nor long by position, it is short.

For example, here is the first line from Manilius's *Astronomicon*:

carmine dīvīnās artēs et cōnscia fātī

As you scan the line, first find the vowels that are long by nature: the *i*'s and the *a* in *dīvīnās*, the *e* in *artēs*, the *o* in *cōnscia*, and the *a* in *fātī* (the *i* is long too, but traditionally the anceps is used regardless.)

NB

An "anceps" is a syllable that can be short or long. It will most often be seen at the end of a line.

Next find the vowels that are long by position: the *a* in *carmine*, the *a* in *artēs*, and the *e* in *et*.

Everything else is short: the *i* and *e* in *carmine*, the *i* and *a* in *cōnscia*.

The fully scanned line looks like this:

$$\text{— ˘ ˘ — — — — — — ˘ ˘ — ˣ}$$
carmine dīvīnās artēs et cōnscia fātī

These aren't just random syllables; there's a rhyme and reason to their arrangement, as explained further in this chapter's rudimentary sketch of poetic theory.

POETIC FEET

Each line of poetry is made up of "feet," or combinations of long and short syllables. The relationship between long and short is roughly equivalent to the relationship between quarter and eighth notes in music.

iamb: (˘ —) short-long.

trochee: (— ˘) long-short

dactyl: (— ˘ ˘) long-short-short

anapest: (˘ ˘ —) short-short-long

spondee: (— —) long-long

tribrach: (˘ ˘ ˘) short-short-short

NB

The vowel at the end of a line can be long or short because it is at the end of the line. It is traditionally marked with an *x*.

ELISION

Poets occasionally make use of a special tool called "elision." An elision can occur when a word ends in a vowel and the next word begins with a vowel or *h*.

Elision can also occur when a word ends in *-am, -em, -im, -om, -um*.

Elisions are typically described as a complete omitting of the elided syllable.

I have also read that elisions are a quick pronunciation of the elided syllable with the following syllable, like a grace note in music.

HENDECASYLLABICS

Hendecasyllabics (11 syllables)/hendies are a meter used by Catullus and Martial. Each line consists of 11 syllables and has an interesting driving beat. It is a great first meter to learn since it is a fairly fixed form.

$$\overset{\smile \; —}{— \smile \; — \smile \smile \; — \smile \; — \smile \; — \; x}$$

Variation is possible on the first two syllables only, as shown above..

Catullus wrote many hendecasyllabic poems. Poem 43, which I present here, is one of my favorites for introducing Catullus and hendecasyllabics. The poem flows nicely off the tongue when you recite it, and the subject matter is quite humorous (and thankfully tamer than many of Catullus's other poems!):

$$— \; — \quad — \; \smile \smile \; — \; \smile \; — \smile \; — \; x$$
salvē, nec minimō puella nāsō

Hello, girl neither with the smallest nose

$$— \quad — \; — \; \smile \smile \quad — \; \smile \; — \; \smile \; — \; x$$
nec bellō pede nec nigrīs ocellīs

nor with a pretty foot nor with black eyes

$$— \quad — \; — \; \smile \smile \; — \quad \smile \quad — \smile \; — \; x$$
nec longīs digitīs nec ōre siccō

nor with long fingers nor with a dry mouth

$$— \quad — \; — \; \smile \smile \quad — \smile \; — \; \smile \; — \; x$$
nec sānē nimis ēlegante linguā,

nor [obviously] with too much of an elegant tongue,

$$\_\ \_\ \_\ \cup\ \cup\ \_\ \cup\ \_\ \cup\ \_\ x$$
dēcoctōris amīca Formiānī

girlfriend of the bankrupt Formian guy.

$$\_\ \_\ \_\ \cup\ \cup\ \_\ \cup\ \_\ \cup\ \_\ x$$
tēn prōvincia nārrat esse bellam?

Does the province tell that you are pretty?

$$\_\ \_\ \_\ \cup\ \cup\ \_\ \cup\ \_\ \cup\ \_\ x$$
tēcum Lesbia nostra comparātur?

With you our Lesbia is compared?

$$\_\ \_\ \_\ \cup\ \cup\ \_\ \cup\ \cup\ \_\ \cup\ x$$
ō saeclum īnsapiēns et īnfacētum!

O foolish and witless age!

NB

The "bankrupt Formain guy" is Mamurra, about whom Catullus wrote 6 poems. Formia is a coastal Italian town between Naples and Rome.

I also wanted to include this excerpt from poem 42, because Catullus addressed it to his verses themselves. Unlike in poem 43, you will be able to see the possible variations in the first foot of each line.

$$\cup\ \_\ \_\ \cup\ \cup\ \_\ \cup\ \_\ \cup\ \_\ x$$
adest(e), hendecasyllabī, quot estis
Come hendecasyllabics as many as you are

$$\_\ \_\ \_\ \cup\ \cup\ \_\ \cup\ \_\ \cup\ \_\ x$$
omnēs undique, quotquot es tis omnēs.
Everyone from all sides, however so many you are.

$$\cup\ \_\ \_\ \cup\ \cup\ \_\ \cup\ \_\ \cup\ \_\ x$$
iocum mē putat esse moecha turpis,

That dirty adultress thinks me a joke,

‿ ‿ ‿ ‿ ‿ ‿ ‿ ‿ ‿ ‿ x
et negat mihi nostra redditūram
And denies that she will return to me our

‿ ‿ ‿ ‿ ‿ ‿ ‿ ‿ ‿ ‿ x
pugillāria, sī patī potestis.
Writing tablets, if you are able to endure it.

‿ ‿ ‿ ‿ ‿ ‿ ‿ ‿ ‿ ‿ x
persequāmur e(am) et reflāgitēmus.
We should chase her down and demand them back.

Martial is the only other major Latin writer to write in hendecasyllabics. Similar to Catullus's poems, many of Martial's hendecasyllabic poems are rather long. I have found a few short ones among his many poems so that you can practice with complete poems.

8.5

‿ ‿ ‿ ‿ ‿ ‿ ‿ ‿ ‿ ‿ x
dum dōnās, Macer, ānulōs puellīs,
While you give, Oh Macer, rings to girls,

‿ ‿ ‿ ‿ ‿ ‿ ‿ ‿ ‿ ‿ x
dēsistī, Macer, ānulōs habēre.
You cease, Oh Macer, to have rings.

12.73

‿ ‿ ‿ ‿ ‿ ‿ ‿ ‿ ‿ ‿ x
hērēdem tibi mē, Catulle, dīcis.
You say, Oh Catullus, that I am your heir.

Nōn crēdam, nisi lēgerō, Catulle.

I won't believe it, unless I shall

have read it, Oh Catullus.

NB

Look everyone, it's a future perfect verb, a rare specimen to find in the wild!

The future perfect expresses a time before some time in the future.

lēgerō	I shall have read	**lēgerimus**	**We** shall have read
lēgeris	**You** shall have read	**lēgeritis**	**You all** shall have read
lēgerit	**He/She/It** shall have read	**lēgerint**	**They** shall have read

In this case Martial says that in the impossible future in which he would believe Catullus's claim, he would have read it prior to believing it!

14.37

sēlēctōs nisi dās mihi libellōs,

Unless you give me my chosen books,

admittam tineās trucesque blattās!

I will let loose bookworms and fierce moths!

Interestingly, though it was not much used in Classical Latin poetry, hendecasyllabics would go on to become an important meter for Italian poets of the Renaissance.

DACTYLIC HEXAMETER

Dactylic hexameter is the epic meter used by Homer in the *Iliad* and the *Odyssey*, Vergil in the *Aeneid,* and Ovid in the *Metamorphoses*. Juvenal (page 126) and Horace (page 120) wrote in dactylic hexameter in their satires, and the philosopher-poet Lucretius made use of it in his *De rerum natura*.

Dactylic hexameter is made up of six (Greek *hex*) feet, each of which are either dactyls or spondees. Each of the first four feet can be either spondees or dactyls, the fifth foot is always a dactyl, and the sixth foot is always a spondee. Most lines are separated by a brief pause, called a caesura, which is represented by two slashes (//).

$$— — — — / — // — — — — ˘ ˘ — ×$$
$$— ˘ ˘ — ˘ ˘ — // ˘ ˘ — ˘ ˘ — ˘ ˘ — ×$$

These two lines, apparently from Ennius, which name the Olympian gods, is a good illustration of (and provides practice in) dactylic hexameter:

$$— — — ˘ ˘ — ˘ ˘ — // — ˘ ˘ — ×$$
Iūnō Vesta Minervā Cerēs Diāna Venus Mārs

$$— ˘ ˘ — // — — — — // — — ˘ ˘ — ×$$
Mercurius lōvīs Neptūnus Vulcānus Apollō

FAMOUS FIRST LINES OF LATIN POEMS

_ ˇ ˇ _ ˇ ˇ _ // _ _ _ _ ˇ ˇ _ x
arma virumque canō, Troiae quī prīmus ab ōrīs...

Of war I sing and the man who first from the shores of Troy...

—Vergil, *Aeneid* (the book of Aeneas)

_ ˇ ˇ _ ˇ ˇ _ // _ _ _ _ ˇ ˇ _ x
in nova fert animus mūtātās dīcere fōrmās...

The spirit moves me to speak of forms transformed into new things...

—Ovid, *Metamorphoses* (the book of changes)

_ _ _ ˇ ˇ _ // _ _ _ _ ˇ ˇ _ x
Mūsae quae pedibus magnum pulsātis Olympum

Oh you Muses who beat great Olympus with your feet [Get it—like metrical feet?]

—Ennius, *Annales* (annals/history)

_ ˇ ˇ _ ˇ ˇ _ // ˇ ˇ _ _ _ ˇ ˇ _ x
Aeneadum genetrīx, hominum dīvomque voluptās,

O! Aeneas's mother, desire of men and of gods...

—Lucretius, *De rerum natura* (on the nature of things)

_ ˇ ˇ _ _ _ _ _ // _ _ _ ˇ ˇ _ x
semper eg(o) audītor tantum? nūmquamne repōnam

Will I always be one a listener? Will I never repay...?

—Juvenal, *Satire I*

_ _ _ ˇ ˇ _// _ _ _ _ ˇ ˇ _ x
hūmānō capitī ceruīcem pictor equīnam

A painter (should she want to join) the neck of a horse with the head of a human...

—Horace, *Ars poetica* (the art of poetry)

$$\_ \, \smallsmile\smallsmile \, \_ \quad \_ \quad \_ \, // \, \_ \quad \_ \quad \_ \quad \_ \, \smallsmile\smallsmile \, \_ \quad x$$
Pēliacō quondam prōgnātae vertice pīnus

Once upon a time pines born on the top of Mount Pelion . . .

    —Catullus 64

$$\_ \quad \smallsmile \, \smallsmile \quad \_ \quad \smallsmile \quad \smallsmile \, \_ \, // \, \_ \quad \_ \, \smallsmile \quad \smallsmile \quad \_ \, \smallsmile\smallsmile \quad \_ \quad x$$
omnia, Castor, emis. sīc fīet ut omnia vēndās.

You buy everything, Castor. And so it will happen that you will sell it all.

    —Martial 7.98

ELEGAIC COUPLETS

This meter is interesting because of the way its second line employs stops:

$$\_ \, \overline{\smallsmile\smallsmile} \, \_ \, \overline{\smallsmile\smallsmile} \, \_ \, // \, \overline{\smallsmile\smallsmile} \, \_ \, \overline{\smallsmile\smallsmile} \, \_ \, \smallsmile \, \smallsmile \, \_ \, x$$
$$\_ \, \overline{\smallsmile\smallsmile} \, \_ \, \overline{\smallsmile\smallsmile} \, \_ \, // \, \_ \, \smallsmile\smallsmile \, \_ \, \smallsmile\smallsmile$$

The first line is the same as the dactylic hexameter line discussed above. The second line is made up of two parts: the first has variety, two dactyls or spondees followed by a single long syllable; the second has no variety, two dactyls followed by a single long syllable. This line technically has five feet, but one of them has been split and divided to end each of the two parts.

Catullus 105 is a good example of a brief poem written in this meter. In it Catullus is addressing Mamurra, whom he calls Mentula, which translates into a not-so-nice word, so we will use prick as a euphemism. In this one, he tells us what happened when Mentula tries his hand at poetry (note the use of *scandere*, from which the term "scansion" comes):

$$\_ \; \smile \; \smile \; \_ \; \_ \; \_ \; // \; \_ \; \_ \; \_ \quad \_ \; \smile \; \smile \quad \_ \qquad \mathsf{x}$$
Mentula cōnātur Piplēium scande re montem,

$$\_ \; \_ \quad \_ \; \_ \; \_ // \; \_ \; \smile \; \smile \; \_ \qquad \smile \; \smile \quad \mathsf{x}$$
Mūsae furcillīs praecipit(em) ēiciunt.

Mentula tries to climb the Pipleian mountain;
the Muses throw him down headlong with pitchforks.

Catullus 93, addressed to Julius Caesar, is another complete poem in one elegiac stanza:

$$\_ \quad \smile \; \smile \; \_ \quad \smile \; \smile \; \_ // \; \_ \quad \_ \quad \smile \; \smile \quad \_ \; \smile \; \smile \; \_ \qquad \mathsf{x}$$
nīl nimium studeō, Caesar, tibi velle placēre

$$\_ \qquad \_ \quad \_ \; \_ \qquad \_ // \_ \smile \quad \smile \quad \_ \; \smile \quad \smile \; \_$$
nec scīr(e) ūtrum sīs albus an āt er homō.

In no way am I very much eager, Caesar, to want to please you,
nor to know whether you are a white or dark man.

Ovid is best known for his epic *Metamorphoses*, but most of his works are written in elegiac couplets, including the *Amores*, the *Tristia*, *Ex ponto*, and *Ars amortoria* (the art of love), a controversial love manual with instructions for men on how to woo women (and for women to resist their advances!). As he says in the first two lines:

$$\_ \quad \smile \; \smile \quad \_ \quad \_ \; \_ \; // \; \smile \; \smile \; \_ \quad \_ \; \smile \quad \smile \; \_ \; \_$$
sīquis in hoc artem populō nōn nōvit amandī,

$$\_ \quad \smile \; \smile \quad \_ \quad \_ \_ // \_ \; \smile \; \smile \quad \_ \quad \smile \quad \_$$
hoc legat et lectō carmine doctus amet!

If anyone in this population doesn't know the art of loving,
let them read this and, the song being read, when they are learned,
let them love!

Ovid also wrote the *Heroides*, a collection of 21 short songs sung by the heroines of classical mythology. The first is from Penelope to Ulysses and begins with this stanza:

$$— \ \smile\smile — \smile\smile — // — — \smile\smile — \smile — \smile - \text{x}$$

haec tua Pēnelope lentō tibi mittit, Ulix e

$$— \ \smile\smile — — — // — \smile \ \smile — \smile \ \smile —$$

nīl mihi rescrības attinet: ipse venī!

These words your Penelope sends to you, Oh Ulysses, slowpoke
It doesn't matter should you write back to me: come yourself!

METER CHALLENGE

Put the words in the lines of poetry into the correct order, based on the meter indicated. Make sure to properly place elisions (indicated with parentheses), and remember that the anceps (x) can be short or long!

Hendecasyllables

$$— — — \smile\smile — \smile — \smile — \text{x}$$
$$\smile — — \smile\smile — \smile — \smile — \text{x}$$

1. $\breve{a}$pud mī cēnābis Fabull mē bene
   $$\breve{} — — — — — \smile — \overset{\text{x}}{} \smile\smile\smile$$

2. tibi, diēbus sī dī favent, paucīs
   $$\smile\smile \ \smile - \overset{\text{x}}{} — — \smile — — — —$$

3. bon(am) magnam sī atque attuleris tēc(um)
   $$\smile — \overset{\text{x}}{} — — \smile — \breve{} — \breve{} — — \text{}$$

4. puellā nōn sine, cēnam candidā
   $$\smile - \overset{\text{x}}{} — \smile\smile — — — \smile —$$

5. et cachinnīs vīn(ō) et sal(e) omnibus et
   $$— \smile — \overset{\text{x}}{} — \smile — — — \smile — —$$

Dactylic Hexameter

$$— \smile\smile — \smile\smile — \smile\smile — \smile\smile — \smile\smile — \smile$$

6. quī eī et fluvius vīsus maximus scīlicet,
   $$— — \overset{\text{x}}{} — \smile — — — — \smile\smile — \smile\smile$$

7.
$\bar{\cup}$ — ⏑ — ⏑⏑ — —   — × ⏑⏑ — —
vīdit et quī aliquem ant(e) ingēns maiōrem, nōn

8.
⏑ — ⏑ — ⏑ — ⏑⏑ — × ⏑⏑ — ⏑ ⏑ — ⏑
et dē homōque omnia omnī gener(e) arbor vidētur

9.
— — — — — ⏑⏑ — — × — — ⏑⏑
quisqu(e) vīdit ingentia haec fingit quae maxima

Elegaic Couplets

— ⏑⏑ — ⏑⏑ — // ⏑⏑ — ⏑⏑ — ⏑⏑ — ×
— ⏑⏑ — ⏑⏑ — // — ⏑⏑ — ⏑⏑ —

10.
⏑⏑ — — — ⏑ — × — — — — — ⏑ —
legis dūcis nōn libenter et vultūs ista quī

11.
⏑ — — ⏑ ⏑ — ⏑ ⏑ — — ⏑ — ⏑ ⏑
tibī līvide invideās nēmo omnibus

ANSWERS

Catullus 13.1-5

1.
— — — ⏑ ⏑ — ⏑ — ⏑ — — ×
cēnābis bene mī Fabull(e) apud mē
You will dine well, my Fabullus, at my house

2.
— — — ⏑ — ⏑ — ⏑ — ×
paucīs, sī tibi dī favent, diēbus
in a few days, if the gods favor you

3.
— — — ⏑ ⏑ — ⏑ — ⏑ — ×
sī tēc(um) attuleris bon(am) atque magnam
if with you you shall have brought a good and big

4.
— — — ⏑⏑ — ⏑ — ⏑ — —
cēnam, nōn sine candidā puellā
dinner, not without a bright girl

5. ēt vīn(ō) ēt săl(e) ĕt ŏmnĭbŭs căchīnnīs

And wine and wit and all the laughs.

Lucretius, *De rerum natura* VI.674

6. scīlicĕt ĕt flŭvĭŭs quī vīsŭs māxĭmŭs ĕī,

And clearly the river which seems biggest to one

7. quī nōn ānt(e) ălĭquĕm măĭōrĕm vīdĭt, ĕt īngēns

who has not seen something bigger before, and a

8. ārbŏr hŏmōquĕ vĭdētŭr ĕt ŏmnĭă dē gĕnĕr(e) ŏmnī

tree and person seem large and everything from every type

9. māxĭmă quae vīdĭt quĭsqu(e), haēc īngēntĭă fīngĭt.

the biggest which each one sees, they think these are big.

Martial I.40

10. quī dūcĭs vūltūs ĕt nōn lĕgĭs ĭstă lĭbēntĕr

You who draw your face and don't read those things gladly

11. ōmnĭbŭs ĭnŭĭdĕās, līuĭdĕ, nēmŏ tĭbī

You should envy everyone, jealous one, no one should envy you.

V

PLAYING AROUND
IN LATIN

LŪDĪ RŌMĀNĪ
(ROMAN GAMES)

Whenever there's talk about games in Roman culture, you usually hear about the large public spectacles that took place in arenas, amphitheaters, and circuses. We're talking some pretty awesome stuff, like gladiator fights, hunts, and chariot races. But in reality, most ancient Romans just watched these games. Believe or not, just as you may not be a Formula One competitor, not every Roman was a chariot racer.

However, this doesn't mean that the non-gladiators didn't have a lot of fun. The games in this chapter are the kind that normal people like you and me would actually participate in. These were games played by children and by soldiers, in back alleys and in bars, for fun and for money.

How do we know what the Romans did in their free time? We know about these games because of archaeological evidence. Game boards have been found, along with playing pieces and die. Even though the rules were not always officially written down, archaeologists have explored how the games might have been played.

In this chapter, I give a description of each game, the original Latin instructions, and some quotes from Latin literature for extra context. You can use these as a fun way to practice Latin with a friend or a group. Remember that your Latin brain will be strengthened by both participation and spectating the games. If possible, do both! Record yourself playing and go back and watch later. The numbers in this chapter, unless otherwise specified, are cardinal numbers, which are explained in the appendix.

TROPĀ

One of the simplest games you can play is called tropā. It consists of players competing to see how many things they can throw into a jar (or any kind of container). It's a fun way of passing the time and practicing your Latin numbers! In the following instructions, the two players are playing with *nuces* (nuts). You can use whatever you'd like to throw: knucklebones, dice, wads of paper, etc. You can play with as many items and as many players as you'd like. To increase the level of difficulty of the game, vary the distance between the jar and the throwers and choose jars with narrow mouths.

QUŌMODO TROPA LŪDERE

I. prīmus ___ nucēs in ōllam
iacere temptat.

II. dēnumerā nucēs in ōllā
prīmō.

III. secundus ___ nucēs in
ōllam iacere temptat.

IV. dēnumerā nucēs in ōllā
secundō.

V. cuuis numerus nucium in
ōllā maior est victor/victrīx.

HOW TO PLAY TROPĀ

I. Player 1 tries to throw ___
nuts into a jar.

II. Count up the number of
nuts in the jar for player 1.

III. Player 2 tries to throw ___
nuts into the jar.

IV. Count up the number of
nuts in the jar for player 2.

V. Whosever number of nuts
in the jar is larger is the
winner.

Though the game is described in various places in English, I have yet to find a description of it in Greek or Latin. I did find Martial's use of the word tropā in 4.14.7-9. Poem 4.14 is addressed to a certain Sinius, and it implores the young man to spend his winter break wisely, reading and not playing games. His lines suggest that it might have been common to play tropā with knucklebones (page 65).

dum blanda vagus āleā December	while a wandering December with a seductive dice
incertīs sonat hinc et hinc fitillīs	resounds here and there in uncertain dice-boxes
et lūdit tropā nēquiōre tālō.	and plays tropā with the rather worthless knucklebone.

December is specifically mentioned because gambling was permitted during this month. At all other times, casting lots was a forbidden activity (though it most certainly still went down, but was just kept on the DL).

MICĀTIŌ

The next time you have to decide who gets the front seat or the last slice of pizza, you could play "rock, paper, scissors" (*saxum, charta, forficēs*), or you could play *micātiō*, which is like "rock, paper, scissors" on steroids. *Micātiō* (also known as *digitōrum*) is a hand game that is best translated into English as "flash fingers."

This game is still played today. It is now called *morra* and is a pastime in various regions of the former Roman Empire. *Morra* is especially popular in Italy, where there is even an Italian Fingers Championship (IFC) group, which was started in 2005 and holds an annual tournament. You can find rules, videos, and information about enrolling in the tournament on the IFC's interestingly titled website, showtimewrestling.com. *Morra* is also popular in Italian American societies.

It is easy enough to play and is also another good way to practice your numbers without mindlessly counting things (which I have subjected many a class to—sorry!). In order to predict the total number of fingers, you will need to call out a cardinal number (see the appendix). You can play with however many people or hands you wish, increasing the highest number depending on the number of hands in play.

You can play up to however many points you and your opponent(s) decide on. The IFC calls for teams of four and games that are split into three rounds (legs), with 12 matches per round. During each match, a member from one team battles a member from the other team, predicting sums from 2 to 10. All members take turns.

QUOMODO MICARE	HOW TO PLAY FLASH FINGERS
I. tollite manum.	I. Raise your hand.
II. dīvīnāte (quid summa digitōrum it aut utrum pār an impār sit)	II. Predict (what the sum will be or whether the sum will be even or odd).
III. extendite digitōs.	III. Show your fingers.
IV. facite summam digitōrum.	IV. Add up all the fingers.
V. quī rēctē dīvīnāvit, pūnctum recipit sī nēmō rēctē dīvīnāvit, lūde iterum.	V. Who guessed correctly gets a point. If no one guessed correctly, play again.
VI. quī ___ pūncta recipit victor/victrīx est.	VI. Whoever receives ___ points is the winner.

According to Gesneri's *Novus linguae Latinae thesaurus*, "micāre digītīs est lūsūs genus quōddam aut sortis" (flashing with the fingers is a certain type of game or casting of lots). Forcellini's *Lexicon* says, "micāre est sortīrī digitīs" (that to play flash fingers is to cast lots with the fingers). In *De divinatione* 2.85, Cicero puts *micātiō* on the same level as knucklebones and dice: "quid enim sors est? īdem prope modum quod micandō, quod tālōs iacere, quod tesserās..." (For what is casting lots? Near the same manner which [there is] in playing micatio, which [there is] to throw the knucklebones, which [there is to throw] dice ...). And last, Cicero, in *De officiis* 3.77, describes a man as "quīcum in tenebrīs micēs" (one with whom you could play micātiō in the dark). This is a proverbial way to describe a player who is really honest; so much so that the player wouldn't lie about how many fingers they were holding up.

ĀLEAE/TESSERAE/TĀLĪ

The word *āleae* (dice) seems to refer to any kind of die. In Roman gaming, there were two main types of dice: *tesserae* (what we call dice) and *tālī* (knucklebones); see page 70. *Tesserae* could be used to play other games, but they could also be used to play with on their own. Ovid tells us in the *Tristia*:

sunt aliīs scrīptae, quibus āleā lūditur, artēs:	The arts, by which dice is played, have been written down by others:
hōc est ad nostrōs nōn leve crīmen avōs	this is no light crime to our grandfathers
tessera quōs habeat numerōs	(and) what numbers a die has

The noun forms of the numbers are used to indicate the numbers on the dice:

ūniō: one	quaterniō: four
bīniō: two, deuce	quīniō: five
terniō: three	sēniō: six

QUOMODO ALEA LUDERE / HOW TO PLAY DICE

QUOMODO ALEA LUDERE	HOW TO PLAY DICE
I. prīmus tesseram/tesserās iacit.	I. Player 1 throws a die/the dice.
II. secundus tesseram/tesserās iacit.	II. Player 2 throws a die/the dice.
III. cuius numerus maior est victor.	III. Whose number is bigger is the winner.

The historian Livy tells us that two consuls, Cloelius and Roscius, were killed after being distracted "in tesserārum prōsperō iactū" (in the favorable throw of the dice) (14.17). Dice were referenced in speech in nongaming contexts and represented fate and chance. The imperial biographer Seutonus reported that Julius Caesar said the following before he crossed the Rubicon river, essentially declaring war on Rome: "ālea iacta est" (the die has been cast). Plutarch, however, reported that Julius Caesar made this very well known remark in Greek.

Fate and chance and their relationship with the lives of humans are major themes explored in Latin literature. Terence (page 122), in the *Adelphoi* (4.7.2fa1), made this interesting comparison between life and dice:

ita uītast hominum, quasi quom lūdās tesserīs:	Thus is the life of people, just like when you play with dice:
sī illud quod maximē opus est iactū nōn cadit,	if that which is greatly needed does not fall with the throw,
illud quod cecidit forte, id arte ut corrigās.	that which did fall by chance, you must correct it by skill.

TĀLĪ/ASTROGALOI

Tālī (*astrogaloi* in Greek) were originally the knucklebones of sheep, which are four sided. Sometimes numbers were put onto *tālī*, but because each of the four sides is a distinguishable shape, they weren't necessary. If numbers were put on, they were 1, 3, 4, and 6. Later knucklebones were made out of various materials to mimic this shape. Today you can buy replica tali from a few outlets, or even print your own on a 3-D printer.

Depending on the luck of the throw, you either get to put money into the pot or get to take money out. Our evidence for this comes from a letter quoted by Suetonius, which was written by the emperor Augustus to his son Tiberius. We know that Augustus had a little bit of a gambling problem, and Suetonius tells us he was in the habit of gambling outside the month of December, on other holidays and non-holidays. In the letter he tells Tiberius that with every *canis* ("dog," a one) or *seniō* (six) you threw, you had to put one coin into the pot. The goal was to roll a "Venus," which happened when all four knucklebones displayed a different side (a one, three, four, and six). The player who rolled a Venus got to take all the coins. More modern incarnations of knucklebones are played like jacks, where you throw a rubber ball and try to pick up a certain number of knucklebones before catching the ball again. This game can be played with three tesserae or four *tālī*.

QUOMODO TĀLĪS LUDERE	HOW TO PLAY TĀLĪ
I. quattuor tālōs iace!	I. Throw four knucklebones!
II. sī canem (ūniōnem) aut sēniōnem mīsistī, dēpōne nummum.	II. If you have thrown a dog (a one) or a six, put down a coin.
III. sī Venerem (ūniōnem et terniōnem et quaterniōnem et sēniōnem) mīsistī, sūme nummōs!	III. If you have thrown a Venus (a one and a three and a four and a six), take the coins!
IV. sī nec canem nec Venerem Venus nec sēniōnem mīsistī, tālōs iace iterum!	IV. If you have thrown neither a dog nor a six, throw the dice again!

V. nummīs omnibus captīs | V. When you have taken all the
(aut tuīs āmīsistis), | coins (or lost all yours), stop
dēsiste. lūdendō. | playing.

Augustus wasn't the only emperor addicted to playing dice (though it seems a harmless vice compared to those of other Roman emperors). Seutonius says of Claudius: "āleam studiōsissimē lūsit, dē cuius arte librum quoque ēmīsit, solitus etiam in gestātiōne lūdere, ita essedō alueōque adaptātīs nē lūsus cōnfunderētur." (He played dice with great zeal, about the art of which he also published a book, he was accustomed to playing even when being in the chariot and he played in a carriage adapter with a game board in such a way that the game wouldn't be disturbed.)

The supposed book about dice written by the emperor Claudius is unfortunately lost to history.

In his essay on the joys of old age, Cicero says: "Therefore let others have weapons for themselves, horses for themselves, spears for themselves, swimming and running for themselves, they should leave to us old folks from their many games knucklebones and dice, do that only as it is pleasing, because without them old age is able to be blessed."

LATRUNCULĪ

The word *latrunculī* means "highwaymen" or "brigands." In the context of gaming, it can mean "pawns." This strategy game is most often compared with chess and is comparable to a rudimentary version of the Chinese strategy game Go.

NB

Various names have been used for the playing piece: *latrō* or *mīles* (soldier) and *bellātor* (warrior). Some have taken this to mean that there are different pieces with differing roles (as in modern chess). Some depictions of *latrunculī* on the Internet depict an extra pyramid-looking shape. According to Schadler, however, there was no distinction between the pieces (like checkers with no kings). We will use all the same pieces in our version for simplicity's sake. The sizes of the game boards found by archeologists have varied, but you can play on a modern checkers board with checkers pieces.

I. locāte vagōs invicem.

I. Place pieces in turns.

II. vagīs locātīs, movē vagōs tuōs. vagī movērī ūnum spatium (ad dextram, ad sinistrum, rūrsus, prōrsus) an vagōs aliōs trānsaltāre possunt.

II. With the pieces placed, move your pieces. The pieces can be moved one space (to the right, to the left, backward, forward) or can jump over other pieces.

III. sī vagōrum ūnus est inter vagōs adversāriī duōs alligātus est et conversus.

III. If one of your pieces is between two of your opponent's pieces, it is "bound" and turned over.

IV. sī ūnus alligātōrum ā vagīs alligārī duīs potest, vagus servātus est. sī ūnus alligātōrum nōn alligārī potest, vagus captus est.

IV. If one of your opponent's pieces binding your piece can itself be bound by two of your pieces, your piece is saved. If one of those pieces cannot be bound, your piece is captured by your opponent.

V. quī vagum ūnum habet est perditor

V. The player who has one piece is the loser.

In the same passage from the *Tristia* above, Ovid continues describing what seems to be a game of latrunculi:

[sunt aliīs scrīptae artēs . . .]

[There are other arts written by others . . .]

discōlor ut rēctō grassētur līmite mīles,

how the multicolored soldier advances in a straight line,

cum medius geminō calculus hoste perit

while a piece is being lost in the middle of the twin enemy,

ut bellāre sequēns sciat et reuocāre priōrem,

how one pursuing knows to attack and to call back a piece in front,

nec tūtō fugiēns incomitātus eat;	and how it does not go fleeing into safety unaccompanied;
parva sit ut ternīs īnstrūcta tabella lapillīs,	how a small board is arranged with three stones each,
in quā vīcisse est continuāsse suōs;	on which to have won is to have united ones pieces;

XII SCRĪPTŌRUM

lūdus duōdecim scrīptōrum (the game of XII letters) is similar to backgammon. The game is played on three rows of 12 spaces, usually made up of two six-letter words per row that make up a phrase or even a menu for a restaurant or bar! The variant of words below is based on what could have been a board that was found inscribed into the ground in the forum at Timgad, Algeria, in North Africa: "vēnārī lavārī lūdere rīdēre ōccest vīvere vivere" (hunting, bathing, playing, laughing, this is living).

The words are set up on the board in the following fashion:

VĒNĀRĪ	LAVĀRĪ
LŪDERE	RĪDĒRE
ŌCCEST	VĪVERE

Traditional rules say that two players must try to get 15 pieces from start to finish, though it is uncertain exactly what the rules and the path of the pieces really were. One board from Ostia, the Roman port town, is used by many to establish the path of the pieces:

```
CCCCCC                BBBBBB

AAAAAA1               AAAAAA2

DDDDD                 EEEEE
```

According to instructions interpreted by HJR Murray, the line of As on the left is the home base for one player's pieces, and the line of As on the right is the home base for the other player's pieces. Players throw three dice at a time to move their pieces down the line, until all their pieces have made it off the board at E. If one of your opponent's pieces lands on a space with only one of your pieces, you must restart that piece at the beginning; if the space has more than one of your pieces, your opponent has to restart his or her piece.

Another clever option for a *duodecim scriptorum* board is the following:

```
LEVĀTĒ                DĒLOCŌ

LŪDERE                NESCĪS

IDIŌTA                RECĒDE
```

Which translates as, "Raise yourself from your spot; you don't know how to play, idiot, depart!"

VI

LATIN SONGS

If you google "learn Spanish songs," you will be taken to many sites and videos featuring a variety of songs and music that can supplement your learning of the Spanish language. If you change "Spanish" to "Latin," you will be taken to many sites featuring songs about Latin grammar, which are mostly written for Latin students to help them memorize verb and noun paradigms. You might get the impression that there are no songs in Latin, but they do exist. You just have to know where to find them.

A Roman would be confused by what I just said. A Roman would object and say: "You have plenty of examples of Latin songs in your book! Songs from Catullus and Vergil and Martial!" This is because Latin poets referred to their works as *carmina* (songs) and to the activity they were engaging in as *canere* (singing). However, it is unclear what precise role music had in relation to poetry. It is thought that some musical accompaniment was played during poetic recitations, similar to the medieval bard with his lyre. But no Latin sheet music or musical instructions have been found that would indicate to a performer what to play (unless the performer played standard patterns, like those found in modern blues, or improvised).

First, a multitude of choral works have been written in Latin over the centuries that are readily accessible online. I have had many students who were in choir come to me, proud that they were able to understand some of the Latin they were practicing for their performances (they also would tell me they're "pronouncing it wrong" because the songs are sung in an Ecclesiastical pronunciation). I recently talked to a parent volunteer who attends Catholic Mass and she told me that her mom knows all the Latin words to hymns by heart, but doesn't know any Latin. If music can help a person remember Latin even though he or she doesn't understand it, just imagine how singing Latin songs can help someone who does!

Like I said in Chapter IV, rhythm is a powerful aide in memorizing, and so is melody. Your Latin brain will grow by singing and listening to songs. Hopefully, some of them will become earworms that are stuck on repeat in your head (sorry!). I have picked Latin songs that I hope will be comprehensible to many readers. You can look the melodies up very easily on Google so that you can start singing along.

NB

You might notice that in some poems and lyrics, Latin letters appear in parentheses. This is to account for elision—these letters may be necessary for spelling, but not always for speaking or singing.

STANDARDS

It's helpful to know a few old standbys. Here are some songs you probably know by heart that will be very understandable and fun to sing.

ABECEDĀRIUM: THE ALPHABET

Here is a version of the ABCs I used to sing with my elementary-school students. It's sung to the tune of "O My Darling Clementine." The last line means "These are the Latin letters."

ā, bē, cē, dē,
ē, ef, gē, hā,
ī, kā, el, em, en, ō, pē
qū, er, es, tē
ū, x, y, z
literrae sunt Latīnae

HAPPY BIRTHDAY

fēlīcem nātālem tibi!	Happy Birthday to you!
fēlīcem nātālem tibi!	Happy Birthday to you!
fēlīcem nātālem, cārus/cāra ___!	Happy Birthday, dear ___!
fēlīcem nātālem tibi!	Happy Birthday to you!

As I was researching Latin versions of these songs, I found out some interesting information. Believe it or not, "Happy Birthday" came into the public domain only in 2016 after a legal battle between a documentarian and the Warner/Chappell music publisher, who owned the rights to the 1935 song. Otherwise, I wouldn't have been able to include the song for free, which seems silly for such a simple song.

TWINKLE, TWINKLE, LITTLE STAR

The following translation of "Twinkle, Twinkle, Little Star" is found in Latin schoolbooks from the late 19th and early 20th centuries:

micā, mīca, parva stella!	Shine, shine, little star!
mīror quaenam sīs, tam bella!	I wonder what you are, so beautiful!
splendēns ēminus in illō	Shining from a distance in that
alba velut gemma, caelō.	Sky, just like a white jewel.

But did you know there are more verses?

auandō fervēns Sōl discessit,	When the blazing Sun departs,
nec calōre prāta pāscit,	And does not feed the meadows with warmth
mox ostendis lūmen pūrum,	Soon you show your pure light,
micāns, micāns per obscūrum	Shining, shining through the darkness
tibi, noctū quī vagātur,	The one who roams at night is grateful,
ob scintillulam grātātur;	To you because of your little spark;
nī micārēs tū, nōn scīret	If you did not shine, he would not know
quās per viās errāns īret	Along which roads he should go a-wandering

meum saepe thalamum lūce	Often you look at my bedroom
speculārīs cūriōsa;	With a curious light;
neque carpserīs sopōrem	Nor shall you have captured sleep
dōnec venit Sōl per auram.	Until the Sun has come through the air.

In 1806, Jane Taylor wrote the original English version (not included here) based on the melody of a French song that has even more interesting lyrics, "Ah, vous dirai-je, maman."

tibi dīcam, Ō, māter	Shall I tell you, O, mother
quā dē caus(ā) ego vexer?	Why I am bothered?
pater m(ē) in mod(ō) adultī	Father wants me to reason
vult ratiōcinārī	In the manner of an adult
nūgās valer(ē) adfirmem	I should affirm that trifles are
plūs quam ratiōnem.	More important than reason.

I'VE BEEN WORKING ON THE RAILROAD

cotīdiē labōrāvī	Every day I've been working
viā trāminis	On the train road
cotīdiē labōrāvī	Every day I've been working
ut tempus perdam.	To waste the time.
nōnne tintinābul(um) audīs	Don't you hear the signal-bell?

manē ut surgēmus?	So that we'll get up in the morning?
cotīdiē labōrāvī	Every day I've been working
viā trāminis.	On the train road.

THE EYES OF TEXAS

The school song for the University of Texas, my *alma māter*, is "The Eyes of Texas," which is sung to the tune of "I've Been Working on the Railroad." I would be remiss if I did not include a copy of this song in Latin as a tribute to the institution that made it possible for me to be here today:

NB

alma māter, a Latin phrase meaning "nourishing mother," is a term of endearment used to refer to your high school and/or college.

oculī Texiae tē spectant	The eyes of Texas are watching you
semper cotīdiē	Always, every day
oculī Texiae tē spectant	The eyes of Texas are watching you
nōn potes fugere	You cannot run away
nē putēs tē effugere	Don't think that you'll escape
nocte an manē	By night or in the morning

oculī Texiae tē spectant	The eyes of Texas are watching you
dum sonātur tuba.	Until the horn sounds.

SONGS WRITTEN IN LATIN

LALLA, LALLA, LALLA

This simple song is supposed to go all the way back to the ancient Romans and is the only song I can find that can make this claim. *The Oxford Book of Latin Verse* lists it as "An Ancient Lullaby Anonymous (Incertae Aestatis – Of an uncertain time period)":

Lalla, lalla, lalla	Lala, lala, lala
aut dormī aut lactā	Either sleep or nurse

DĒ BREVITĀTE VĪTAE

This is one of the more popular and familiar songs in Latin and is more commonly known by the first two words *gaudeāmus igitur* (let's rejoice then). I have seen it described as a graduation song, an academic drinking song, or a feast-time song. Though it has a lighthearted melody, its topic is deeper than you might expect for an academic song and reflects a thematic thread that goes back through the Latin poets. Horace's *carpe diem* (seize the day) is the best example of this theme, based on the philosophy of the Greek philosopher Epicurus. This philosophy calls for its adherents to enjoy life while they are alive, because death will come to all. Epicureans don't, however, advocate hedonism, but instead moderation in all things. The Roman writer and Stoic philosopher Seneca also wrote an essay called "dē brevitāte vītae" (on the shortness of life).

gaudeāmus igitur,	Let's rejoice then,
iuvenēs dum sumus;	While we are young;
post iūcundam iuventūtem,	After pleasing youth,
post molestam senectūtem	After troublesome old age
nōs habēbit humus,	The ground will have us,
nōs habēbit humus.	The ground will have us.
ubi sunt, quī ante nōs	Where are they, those who before us
in mundō fuēre?	Were in the world?
vādite ad superōs,	Go to the gods,
trānsīte ad īnferōs,	Go over to the lowest parts,
ubi iam fuēre,	Where they have been already,
ubi iam fuēre.	Where they have been already.
vīta nostra brevis est,	Our life is brief,
brevī fīniētur;	Soon it will be finished;
venit mors vēlōciter,	Death comes swiftly,
rapit nōs atrōciter;	It takes us fiercely;
nēminī parcētur,	It will be spared for none,
nēminī parcētur.	It will be spared for none.
pereat trīstitia,	Let sadness die,
pereant ōsōrēs,	Let haters die,

pereat diabolus	Let the devil die,
quīvīs antiburschius,	Whoever is anti-student,
atque irrīsōrēs.	And the mockers.

The Escorts, a 1950s rock band from Cedar Rapids, Iowa, recorded a version of this song that can be found on YouTube. This recording is unique, because I cannot find another doo-wop song originally recorded in Latin.

There is also a scene from *The West Wing* in which White House staffers sing "Gaudeāmus igitur."

FLĒVIT LEPUS PARVULUS

The following song, told from the point of view of a rabbit, is said to have been popular with students of Latin once upon a time. A 1916 *Handbook for Latin* refers to it as a "16th century student song." The music website Mama Lisa's World (mamalisa.com) traces it back to 12th-century Germany. There are more lyrics to this song, but I opted not to include them, as they are about eating the rabbit at a feast.

flēvit lepus parvulus clāmāns altīs vōcibus:	The wee-little hare wept Shouting with deep voices:
chorus quid fēcī hominibus, quod mē sequuntur canibus?	What did I do to the humans, That they're following me with dogs?
neque in hortō fuī neque holus comēdī.	Neither was I in the garden Nor did I eat a vegetable.

(repeat chorus)

| longās aurēs habeō | I have long ears |
| brevem caudam teneō | I have a short tail |

(repeat chorus)

| levēs pedēs habeō | I have light feet |
| magnum saltum faciō | I do a large jump |

(repeat chorus)

| domus mea silva est | My home is the forest |
| lectus meus dūrus est | My couch is hard |

(repeat chorus)

CARMINA BURANA

The *Carmina burana* is a collection of more than 250 poems written in Medieval Latin and German. In 1936, the composer Carl Orff used 24 of these poems as a basis for his pieces. Orff placed his *Carmina Burana* in a triptych, including a piece using poems of Catullus and a piece describing a wedding ceremony. The most recognizable movement from Orff's *Carmina Burana* is called "Fortūna Imperātrīx Mundī" (Fortune, empress of the world). In fact, you have probably heard this dramatic piece in film trailers, though you might not recognize it by its name (go look it up—I'll wait). However, I have included another song from the *Carmina Burana* that Orff also used in his work. Though its content is a little scurrilous, its Seussian quality is amusing and hard to find in Latin (outside of translations of Dr. Seuss books).

| in tabernā quandō sumus, | When we're in the bar, |
| nōn cūrāmus quid sit humus, | We don't care what the ground is, |

sed ad lūdum properāmus,	But we hasten to the gaming table,
cui semper īnsūdāmus.	Which we always sweat on.
quid agātur in tabernā,	What happens in the tavern,
ubi nummus est pincerna,	Where the coin is a cupbearer,
hoc est opus ut querātur,	This needs to be asked,
sed quid loquar, audiātur.	But what I'm going to say needs to be heard.
quīdam lūdunt, quīdam bibunt,	Some play, some drink,
quīdam indiscrētē vīvunt;	Some live indiscriminately;
sed in lūdō quī morantur,	But from those who delay at the gaming table,
ex hīs quīdam dēnūdantur,	Some are naked,
quīdam ibi vestiuntur,	Some there are clothed,
quīdam saccīs induuntur.	Some are clothed in sacks.
ibi nūllus timet mortem,	There no one fears death,
sed prō Bacchō mittunt sortem.	But they throw their lot for Bacchus.
prīmō prō nummātā vīnī,	At first for the wine merchant,
ex hāc bibunt lībertīnī,	(And because of this one) the freedmen drink,

post haec bibunt ter pro vivis,	One time they drink for the captives,
semel bibunt prō captīvīs,	After these they drink three times for the living,
quater prō Chrīstiānīs cūnctīs,	Four times for all the Christians,
quīnquiēs prō fidēlibus dēfūnctīs,	Five times for the faithful dead,
sexiēs prō sorōribus vānīs,	Six times for the vain sisters,
septiēs prō mīlitibus silvānīs.	Seven times for the forest soldiers.
octiēs prō frātribus perversīs,	Eight times for evil brothers,
noviēs prō monachīs dispersīs,	Nine times for the far-flung nuns,
deciēs prō nāvigantibus,	Ten times for those sailing,
ūndeciēs prō discordantibus,	Eleven times for those quarreling,
duodeciēs prō penitentibus,	Twelve times for those repenting,
tredeciēs prō iter agentibus.	Thirteen times for those making a journey.
tam prō pāpā quam prō rēge	As much for the pope as for the king
bibunt omnēs sine lēge.	Everyone drinks without law.

bibit hera, bibit herus,	The mistress drinks, the master drinks,
bibit mīles, bibit clērus,	The soldier drinks, the cleric drinks,
bibit ille, bibit illa,	He drinks, she drinks,
bibit servus cum ancillā,	The slave drinks with a slave-lady,
bibit vēlōx, bibit piger,	The swift one drinks, the slow one drinks,
bibit albus, bibit niger,	The white one drinks, the black one drinks,
bibit cōnstāns, bibit vagus,	The constant one drinks, the wanderer drinks,
bibit rudis, bibit magus.	The ignorant one drinks, the magician drinks.
bibit pauper et aegrōtus,	The poor one and the sick one drink,
bibit exul et ignōtus,	The exile and the unknown drink,
bibit puer, bibit cānus,	The boy drinks, the white-haired man drinks,
bibit presul et decānus,	The bishop drinks, the deacon drinks,

bibit soror, bibit frāter,	The sister drinks, the brother drinks,
bibit ānus, bibit māter,	The crone drinks, the mother drinks,
bibit ista, bibit ille,	She drinks, he drinks,
bibunt centum, bibunt mīlle.	100 drink, 1,000 drink.
parum centum sex nummātae	106 wine merchants hardly
dūrant, ubi immoderātē	Last, when everyone
bibunt omnēs sine mētā,	Drinks immoderately without end,
quamvīs bibant mente laeta.	Althrough they drink with a happy mind.
sīc nōs rōdunt omnēs gentēs	For this all peoples slander us
et sīc erimus egentēs.	And for this we will be needy.
quī nōs rōdunt, cōnfundantur	Those who slander us, may they be confounded
et cum iūstīs nōn scrībantur.	And may they not be written about with the just and righteous.

MODERN LATIN SONGS

Though a rare occurrence, original Latin songs have come out in the modern era. In 1972, Cat Stevens (now known as Yusuf Islam) released the song "Ō Cāritās," a hymn to love and compassion in an impermanent world that is burning. The arrangement is reminiscent of flamenco music and is overall very pleasing to listen to. The Latin composition is also well done.

One of the most interesting modern Latin groups is Ista, a German rap group that was started in the 1990s by some bored classics students. Ista illustrates very well how adaptive Latin can be, even into modern musical forms like rap. Ista's original songs address common themes found throughout Latin literature, such as what it means to be a Roman, what it means to be in love, and what it means to be human. The music is definitely an older, more European electronic style of hip-hop than American listeners might be used to, but the experience is still worth it. Especially worth checking out are the band's music videos. There is also a live Ista performance available on YouTube (unfortunately, the audio mix is low quality on this recording). Ista's website (ista-latina.de) has several mp3 singles and albums available for sale.

SONGS TRANSLATED INTO LATIN

Earlier I said that "Gaudeāmus igitur" by the Escorts is the only doo-wop song originally recorded in Latin. I say "originally recorded" because a dozen or so doo-wop songs have been translated into Latin. These were released in the 1990s by a Finnish literature professor whose stage name is Dr. Ammondt. Ammondt also released two albums of Latin translations of Finnish tangos (one of which earned a medal from the Pope) and three rock songs translated into Sumerian. He says the King would have approved. I was very much inspired by Dr. Ammondt's translations. The first one I translated to perform in class was "Calceī glaucī" ("Blue Suede Shoes"), but it was a hybrid of Ammondt's translation and my own (I could find only the chorus online). A performance of this song is available on YouTube.

Lots of other songs translated into Latin are available on YouTube, and many are understandable and fun to listen to. You will even find (mostly metal) songs that are representatives of improper Latin, perhaps by unskilled (or non-) Latinists. "Halloween 2" by the '80s horror punk band Misfits is a good example of this (azlyrics.com calls it "nonstandard" Latin).

Also on YouTube is Keith Massey, who has translated and performed The Beatles "And I Love Her," "Do You Want to Build a Snowman" from the animated film *Frozen*, and Adele's "Hello." An Oxford student named Olivia, whose handle on YouTube is O1ivette, has also done some good translations of popular Disney songs from *Frozen*, *Aladdin*, and *The Lion King*. These arrangements try to capture the feel of the originals. Another group, Rondellus, puts a medieval twist on its translations of Black Sabbath songs. The songs are performed on period instruments and are reminiscent of classical choral songs composed in Latin.

DOMUS SŌLIS ORIENTIS

The first full song that I translated into Latin was the folk song "House of the Rising Sun" (Domus sōlis orientis). I based the arrangement on that by The Animals, which changes the point of view from a young girl who has lost her sweetheart to a young man whose father is a drunk and a gambler. A performance of this song is available on YouTube.

VII

VULGAR LATIN: THE LATIN OF THE PEOPLE

If you are looking to learn how to insult and curse in Latin, you've come to the wrong place. Believe it or not, so-called Vulgar Latin is offensive only to people like Cicero and other stuffy grammar nerds. Speakers of Vulgar Latin are not all that bad, seeing as we know how Latin was supposed to be spoken and how Latin grammar was supposed to work.

Because there is no audio evidence of what the Latin on the street sounded like, we can rely only on writing, but there are very few examples of real Vulgar Latin, which is technically any Latin that is not "good" Latin. In the literary tradition, poets sometimes playfully violate the strict rules of grammar in the process of writing, and writers for the stage include vulgar speech for certain characters for comedic effect.

NB

Vulgar Latin refers to the Latin of the common people (*vulgus*, common people).

The Vulgate Bible refers to an edition of the Bible that was commonly used (*vulgatus*, common, well known). It was written in "good" Latin.

The *Corpus īnscrīptiōnum Latīnārum* (CIL) is a giant collection of Latin inscriptions that have been found all over the Roman world. (A similar collection of Latin inscriptions can be found in Buecheler's Carmina Latina Epigraphica [B].) Many of the inscriptions are from government buildings and funerary monuments, which are great places to find examples of "good" Latin, "bad" Latin, and also Latin abbreviations. But one of the volumes contains inscriptions and graffiti that have been found in the cities of Pompeii and Herculaneum.

On August 24, 79 CE, the volcano Vesuvius essentially blew up in what is known as a Plinian eruption (so called after the Roman writers Pliny: the Younger, who wrote a description of the eruption and aftermath; and the Elder, who died after getting too close to the cloud of poison gas that radiated out from the eruption). The city of Herculaneum was flooded by an avalanche of lava, and the more well known city of Pompeii was covered in a giant pile of ash. This preserved the city in that moment of time for more than a thousand years. When the city was discovered, food was found ready to eat on tables, bodies were found creepily preserved, and walls were covered with the Latin of the people. Some of the latter resembles some bathroom stalls I've seen as a high-school teacher (both in appearance and content!).

EXAMPLES OF VULGAR LATIN

We will start a quick look through examples of Vulgar Latin with an example written on the walls of Pompeii that evaluates the Roman habit of carving and writing on walls. It is up to you to decide if you agree or not:

stultōrum calamī carbōnēs moenia chartae.

Charcoal/chalk are the pens of stupid people, walls their paper.

You will recognize messages similar to those you have doubtless seen (or written) yourself in English.

Q et Salvvīī(?) [sic.] hīc fuērunt.
(CIL #1877)

Quintus and Salvius were here.

There are professions of love:

Mārcellum Fortūnāta cupit
(CIL #111)

Marcellus
Fortunata desires him

Mamius Salius Fōrmōsus
(CIL #G0286)

Mamius Salius
(is) beautiful

And reactions to lost love:

Sarra, nōn bellē facis

Sarah, you are not doing prettily

solum mē relinquis	You are leaving me alone
dēbilis ...	helpless ...
(CIL #1951)	

Some refer to mythological stories:

carminibus	With songs
Circē sociōs	Circe
mūtāvit	changed
olyxis	the comrades of Ulysses
(CIL #1982)	

Some are accompanied with illustrations:

labyrithus	The Labyrinth
hic habitat	here lives
Mīnōtaurus	the Minotaur
(CIL #2331)	

Some pictures of arena fights have been discovered that are accompanied by captions describing the performance of a fighter. This description of a street performer or arena fighter is written in the form a snake:

serpentis lūsūs sī quī sibi forte notāvit	If any snake games, by chance, have been known to you,
Sepumius iuvenis quōs facit ingeniō	the games which the youth Sepumius plays with his talent,
spectātor scaenae sīve es studiōsus equōrum	whether you are a watcher of the stage or fond of horses
sīc habeās lancēs semper ubīque pārēs.	thus you shall have your scales always everywhere equal.

Several interesting examples of graffiti were written to innkeepers (early Yelp reviews?):

miximus in lectō fateor peccāvimus	We peed in the bed, I confess, we messed up.
hospes sī dicēs quārē nūlla matella fuit (CIL IV D4957)	Host, if you say why: there was no chamber pot.
tālia tē fallant utinam mendācia, caupō	Would that such lies deceive you, innkeeper.
tū vēndēs aquam et bibēs ipse merum (CIL IV D3948)	You sell water and you drink yourself the wine.

One of the funniest things I came across is the so-called Room of the Seven Sages, a bathhouse in Ostia (a port town near Rome) that features some well-preserved archaeological remains. Among the remains of the bathhouse is a painting of some Greek philosophers: Solon, Thales, and Cheilon. The philosophers have some interesting but unphilosophical advice:

ut bene cacāret ventrem, palpāvit Solōn.	To poop well, Solon stroked his stomach.
dūrum cacantēs monuit ut nitant Thālēs	Thales advises those pooping a hard one to strain.
uissīre tacitē Chīlōn docuit subdolus.	Cunning Chilon taught how to fart silently.

This room also contains a reference to one of the most interesting implements from the Roman Empire, the sponge on a stick:

verbōsē tibi nēmō dīcit dum	No one speaks verbosely to you
ūtāris xylosphongīō	when you use the sponge on a stick.

Literally, *xylosphongio* means "herb-sponge" or "cotton-sponge," a tool that is thankfully not one we are familiar with, but that every Roman would have been. The sponge on a stick was used in the *foricae* (public toilets), which were large rooms with lots of seats to sit on and... you know... That means that going to the bathroom was a much more social event than many modern bathroom users would be able to tolerate. You not only shared stories with your neighbor, you also shared the sponge on a stick, which was, of course, for cleaning yourself (and everyone else) off. But not to worry; a little stream of water ran along the floor at everyone's feet so that you could clean the sponge off for the next person.

As testament to the bizarre (to us) social world that was the *foricae*, Martial wrote the following poem (11.77) about a certain desperate man named Vacerra:

in omnibus Vacerra quod conclāvibus	Why does Vacerra, in all the bathrooms,
cōnsūmit hōrās et diē tōtō sedet,	Waste his hours and sit the whole day,
cenaturit Vacerra, nōn cacāturit.	Vacerra wants to dine, he doesn't want to poop.

TOMBSTONES

Did you know the Romans also cremated their dead and stored the ashes of a loved one in an urn? Then, they built memorials for the urn: some were simple enclosures, but some were so elaborate that they took up entire rooms, decked out with seating and wall paintings. These memorials, the lavish and the simple, were placed on the outskirts of cities and functioned as a sort of billboard for whatever messages the deceased (or the deceased's family) wished to have carved in stone. They were often addressed to travelers and detailed the accomplishments of the deceased and the wishes and grief of the survivors. Many of these were what are known as *memento mori* (itself a Latin phrase meaning "remember that you will die").

Here are some of the salty sayings some Romans left on their grave stones as an enduring jab to the living:

respice et crēde.	Look back and believe.
sīc est, aliud fierī nōn licet. (CIL D6.29952)	This is it, thus it is; to become otherwise it is not permitted.
viātor, viātor!	Traveler, traveler!
quod tū es, ego fuī; quod nunc sum, et tū eris (CIL D11.6243)	What you are, I was; what I now am, you also shall be.

This one is in the same vein as the previous saying, though more sparsely populated with verbs:

viātor! quod tū, et ego; quod ego, et omnēs. (CIL D8.9913)	Traveler! What you (are), I also (was); what I (am), also all (will be).

quī legis hunc titulum,
mortālem, tē esse mementō.
(B 808)

You who read this title,
remember that you are mortal.

dum vīxī, bibī libenter.
bibitē vōs, quī vīvitis!
(B 243)

While I lived, I drank freely.
Drink you, who live!

quod ēdī bibī, mēcum habeō,
quod relīquī, perdidī.
(B 244)

What I ate and drank, I have it
with me; what I left, I lost.

ulterius nihil est morte neque
ūtilius.
(B 1493)

Nothing is beyond death nor
more useful.

vōs ego nunc moneō, semper
quī vīvitis avārē:

I now warn you all, you who
always live greedily:

nūdus nātur(ā) fuerās ā mātre
creātus,

Naked naturally you were, by
your mother, created,

nūdus eris. obitīs grātia nūlla
datur.
(B 1494)

Naked you will be. To the dead
no thanks is given.

nihil sumus et fuimus
mortālēs. respice lector,

Nothing we are and were,
mortals. Look back reader,

in nihil ab nihilō quam cito
recīdimus.
(B 1495)

Into nothing from nothing, how
quickly we return.

ōlim nōn fuimus, nātī sumus
unde quiētī:

Once we were not, we were
born from the place where we
slept.

nunc sumus ut fuimus, cūra
relicta valē.
(B 1496)

Now we are as we were, take
care, you left behind, good-bye.

crēdō certē nē crās.
(CIL 6.23003)

I believe certainly that there
will not be a tomorrow.

VIII

LATIN JOKES

Despite the stereotype of strict and severe Romans, it is clear from the literature that they loved to laugh and play with words. The jokes are sometimes hard for us to fully understand, because sometimes you just have to be there, but we can at least see that they thought lots of jokes were funny. Some of the jokes do stand the test of time, and you might recognize themes and tropes from these ancient jokes still appearing in modern comedy. The first two sections include examples of jokes, witticisms, and the occasional burn from two Romans writing about developing proper oratory skills. The last section includes translations from Greek into Latin (and then English!) of *the* joke book of the ancient world.

QUINTILIAN

One major source of what the Romans thought about humor and laughter is Quintilian, a first-century teacher from Hispania. Quintilian's major work is *Īnstitūtiō ōrātōria*, a 12-book instruction manual on how to raise an orator from birth. Humor is presented in Book 6 as a topic useful for its potential effects on a judge. In this discussion, Quintilian includes some musings on the philosophy of humor, along with some successful (and unsuccessful) jokes that Romans orators have made. Quintilian says that no one has adequately explained what this mysterious and powerful force of humor is and how to use it, so he spends most of this book trying to do just that.

He says that a funny statement (*rīdiculum dictum*) is:

- **plērumque falsum, semper humile**
  - frequently false, always base

- **saepe ex industriā dēprāvātum**
  - often purposely depraved

- **numquam honōrificum**
  - never honorable

He also gives a good general definition of witty speech:

omnis salsē dīcendī ratiō in eō est, ut aliter quam est rēctum vērumque dīcātur: quod fit tōtum fingendīs aut nostrīs aut aliēnīs persuāsiōnibus aut dīcendō quod fierī nōn potest.

Every type of speaking wittily consists of this: to speak contrary to what is correct and true: this happens in totally misrepresenting either our convictions or another's, or in saying something that can't happen.

Quintilian posits that the inspiration for humor lies "praecipuē positum esse in nātūrā et in occāsiōne." (principally in nature and in opportunity.)

He also says that there are three uses of jokes for an orator:

I. aliēna aut reprēndimus aut refūtāmus ēlevāmus aut repercutimus aut ēlūdimus.	I. We either rebuke or rebut or disparage or retort or mock others.
II. nostra rīdiculē indicāmus et dīcimus aliqua subabsurda.	II. We betray ourselves humorously and we say some rather absurd things.
III. dēcipiendīs exspectātiōnibus, dictīs aliter accipiendīs cēterīs, quae neutram persōnam contingent cēterīs, quae neutram persōnam contingent ideōque ā mē media dīcuntur.	III. Deceiving expectations, by [using] words other than is accepted, and in other things, which deal with neither person and therefore called "intermediate" by me.

Overall, I find Quintilian's instructions on humor in oratory to be very applicable even today, almost two millennia after the *Institutio oratoria* was written. Unfortunately, most of the jokes he includes have to be explained too much to be funny. A few, however, are oddly reminiscent of humor we still see today:

Pedō dē myrmillōne quī rētiārium cōnsequēbātur nec feriēbat "vīvum" inquit "capere vult."

About a myrmillo [heavily armed gladiator] who was following a retiarius [net-fighter gladiator] and wasn't succeeding in killing him, Pedo said: "He wants to catch him alive."

eques Rōmānus, ad quem in spectāculīs bibentem cum mīsisset Augustus quī eī dīceret: "ego sī prandēre volō, domum eō," "tū enim" inquit "nōn timēs nē locum perdās."

The emperor Agustus sent a message to a Roman knight who was drinking at the games: "If I want to have lunch, I go home." The knight said: "Because you aren't afraid that you'll lose your spot."

dīxit M. Vestīnus cum eī nūntiātum esset (aliquem mortuum esse) "aliquandō dēsinet pūtēre."

Marcus Vestinus, when it was announced to him that a certain man had died, said: "Someday he will stop stinking."

A. Vīvius dīxit ferrum in Tuccium incīdisse.

Aulus Vivius said that a sword had fallen on Tuccius [rather than that Tuccius had fallen on his sword].

Augustus, nūntiantibus Terraconēnsibus palmam in ārā eius ēnātam, "appāret" inquit "quam saepe accendātis."

Augustus said to the Terraconians, who were reporting that a palm tree had sprouted on their altar: "It is clear how often you burn [sacrifices on the altar]."

Catulus dīcentī Philippō: "quid lātrās?" "fūrem videō" inquit.

To Philippus saying: "Why are you barking?" Catulus said: "I see a thief." [Catulus can also translate to "puppy."]

"libīdinōsior es quam ūllus spadō."

"You are more lustful than any eunuch."

Acisculum, quia esset pactus, "Pacisculum."

Acisculus, because he settled, was called "Pacisculus" [from *pax*, meaning "peace"].

Placidum nōmine, quod is acerbus nātūra esset, "Acidum."

Placidus by name, because he was by nature acerbic, was called "Acidus."

Turium, cum fūr esset, "Tollium."

Turius, since he was a thief, was called "Tollius" [from *tollere*, meaning "to take"].

illud Afrī: "homō in agendīs causīs optimē vestītus."

This was said of Afer: [He is] a man, when it comes to arguing cases, [who is] excellently dressed."

Quintilian gives various cautions throughout the book, such as to avoid making jokes that can backfire, as happened to Longus Sulpicius:

quī, cum ipse foedissimus esset, ait eum contrā quem iūdiciō līberālī aderat nē faciem quidem habēre līberī hominis: cui respondēns Domitius Afer "ex tuī" inquit "animī sententia, Longe, quī malam faciem habet līber nōn est?"

Who, although he himself was very ugly, told the man he appeared against in a freedom-status trial that he did not have the face of a free man; responding to him, Domitius Afer said: "According to the opinion of your mind, Longus, one who has a bad face is not free?"

hominī nēquam lāpsō et ut adlevārētur rogantī "tollat tē quī nōn nōvit."

A wicked person, to a man who had fallen and who was asking to be picked up: "Let someone pick you up who does not know you."

Afer Dīdiō Gallō, quī prōvinciam ambitiōsissimē petierat, deinde, impetrāta ea, tamquam coāctus querēbātur: "age" inquit "aliquid et reī pūblicae causā."

To Didius Gallus, who was granted office in a province after he had sought it very ambitiously and then complained as if he was forced, Afer said: "Do something also for the sake of the republic."

stultē interrogāverat exeuntem dē theātrō Campātium Titius Maximus an spectāsset. Fēcit Campātius dubitātiōnem eius stultiōrem dīcendō: "(nōn), sed in orchēstrā pilā lūsī."

Titius Maximus had stupidly asked Campatius as he was leaving from the theater whether he had watched something. Campatius made his uncertainty stupider by saying: "No, I was playing ball in the orchestra section."

CICERO

When I first read that Mary Beard, author and presenter of awesome BBC documentaries about Rome, wrote that Cicero was the funniest Roman, I didn't want to believe it. It didn't fit with my conception of Cicero as a stuffy, uptight old man. But the more I read about this famous Roman orator, the more I developed a clearer understanding of him.

In Book 6 of the *Institutio oratoria*, Quintilian cites Cicero frequently in his discussion of humor. In fact, according to Quintilian, Cicero's freedman Tiro was supposed to have compiled a collection of Cicero's jokes (Quintilian says it was *a little* too much), but all three volumes have been lost. Here are some examples from Quintilian of Cicero's wit:

Cicerō audītā falsā Vatīnī morte, cum obvium lībertum eius interrogāsset "rēctēne omnia?" dīcentī "rēctē" "mortuus est!" inquit.

Cicero, when he heard false report of Vatinus's death, when he had asked his freedman on the street: "Is everything alright?" To the freedman, saying: "It's all right," Cicero said: "He's dead!"

Cicerō Vibium Curium multum dē annīs aetātis suae mentientem: "tum ergō cum ūnā dēclāmābāmus nōn erās nātus!"

Cicero said to Vilbius Curius, who was lying a lot about the years of his age: "So therefore when we were practicing speeches together, you had not been born!"

[Cicerō] Fabia Dolābellae dīcente trīgintā sē annōs habēre: "vērum est," inquit, "nam hoc illam iam vīgintī annīs audio."

Cicero, when Fabia was saying to Dolabella that she was 30 years old, said: "It's true, for I've heard her say that for 20 years now."

refert Cicerō dē homine praelongō, caput eum ad fornicem
Fabium offendisse.
Cicero said about a very tall man that he had hit his head on the
Fabian Arch.

refert Cicerō: "quid huic abest nisi rēs et virtūs?"
Cicero said: "What is absent from this man except substance and
virtue?"

"quid hōc Naviō ignāvius?" sevērē Scīpiō;
Severely Scipio said: "What is there more ignorant than this
Navius?"

...at in male olentem "videō mē ā tē circumvenīrī" subrīdiculē
Philippus;
...and Philippus very ridiculously said to someone stinking badly: "I
see that I am being surrounded by you."

ōlim Rusca cum lēgem ferret annālem, dissuāsor M. Servīlius "dīc
mihi," inquit "M. Pīnārī, num, sī contrā tē dīxerō, mihi male dictūrus
es, ut cēterīs fēcistī?" "ut sēmentem fēceris, ita metēs" inquit.
Once when Rusca was bringing his voting-age law, his discourager,
Marcus Servilius, said, "Tell me, Marcus Pinarius, whether, if I shall
have spoken against you, are you going to talk badly to me, as you
did to the others?" Rusca said: "As you shall have sown the seed,
thusly will you reap it."

Scīpiō ille maior Corinthiīs statuam pollicentibus eō locō, ubi
aliōrum essent imperātōrum, turmālis dīxit displicēre.
The older Scipio, to the Corinthians who were promising him a
statue in a place, where there were statues of other commanders,
he said that the people there displeased him.

Crassus apud M. Perpernam iūdicem prō Aculeōne cum dīceret, aderat contrā Aculeō Grātidiānō L. Aelius Lamia, dēfōrmis, ut nōstis; quī cum interpellāret odiōsē, "audiāmus" inquit "pulchellum puerum" Crassus; cum esset arrīsum, "nōn potuī mihi" inquit Lamia "fōrmam ipse fingere, ingenium potuī"; tum hic "audiāmus" inquit "disertum": multō etiam arrīsum est vehementius.

Crassus, when he was speaking for Aculeone in front of judge Marcus Perperna, [saw] Lucius Aelius Lamia (who you know is deformed) [who] was present against Aculeo for Gratidianus; who when Crassus was interrupting and said distastefully: "Let us listen to the pretty boy"; when there was a laugh Lamia said, "I was not able to invent my form for myself, I was able to invent my character"; then Crassus said: "Let's listen to the well-spoken one," there was again, much stronger laughter.

PHILOGELOS

The *Philogelos* has the distinction of being the only surviving ancient joke book, thought to date back to the fourth century CE. Its authorship is attributed to the otherwise unknown authors Hierocles and Philagrius. The *Philogelos* is a relatively small collection of 256 poems, but it still gives us a fascinating insight into the ancient world. With any luck, at some point in the future even more joke books will be found that will add to our still-developing understanding of what made the Romans laugh.

NB

As you read through the jokes, you will notice that each poem features a main character representing some stereotype whose stupidity is being illustrated, either in a description of the character or in their responses to the people they encounter (think "dumb blonde jokes").

The main stereotype throughout the *Philogelos* is the *scholasticus,* an intellectual/academic who is too clever for his own good (sometimes an intellectual is talking to another intellectual for increased comedic effect!). Other stereotypes are represented in characters who are greedy, lazy, misogynistic, envious, promiscuous, and gluttonous. There are even 12 jokes about folks with bad breath. However, at other times, the jokes take a more prejudiced slant, like today's ethnic jokes. The ethnicities that are the targets of the barbs are Sidonians, Abderites, and Kymeans.

The *Philogelos* was originally written in Greek, which was a major language of the Roman Empire. I have translated them into Latin (and also English) from the critical edition of the Greek text prepared by 19th century German scholar Alfred Eberhard. I tried to avoid jokes that rely on plays on Latin words and that are more plot driven. If you want more jokes, you can go online for a free e-book version that includes videos of a standup routine by British comedian Jim Bowen. He performs a full set of jokes from the *Philogelos* to a live audience.

XI. scholasticus volēns vidēre an decōrus sit dormiēns, oculīs clausīs sē in speculō īnspicit.

An intellectual, wanting to see whether he was handsome while sleeping, looked at himself in the mirror with his eyes closed.

XVII. scholasticō sodālis peregrīnātus scrīpsit ut sibi librōs emeret. quī oblītus, illō reditō occurrēns "epistula dē librīs" dīxit, "quam mīsistī, nōn recēpī."

A friend traveling abroad wrote so that the intellectual might buy some books for him. "The letter about the books," [the intellectual] said, "which you sent, I did not receive."

XII. scholasticus amīcō aliquō suō occūrēns eī dīxit: "audīvī tē mortuum esse." quī respondit: "sed mē vīvere vidēs." contrā scholasticus: "quī tamen mihi multum dē tē dīxit crēdibilior erat."

An intellectual, when he ran into some friend of his, said to him: "I heard you were dead." His friend responded: "But you see that I am alive." On the other side, the intellectual said: "But the one who told me a lot about you was more believable."

XXXV. scholasticus inaurēs fūrtīvās mercātus, nē cognōscerētur, illā pice oblināvit.

An intellectual who bought stolen earrings, so that they wouldn't be recognized, covered them with pitch.

XLIX. scholasticus lūnam vidēns, patris rogat an aliīs urbibus eaedem lūnae sint.

The intellectual, seeing the moon, asks his father whether other cities have the same moon.

LV. scholasticus lepidus impēnsīs pauperibus librōs suōs vēndit atque scrībēns ad patrem dīcit: "gaudē mēcum, pater, nam tandem mē librīs meīs nūtriō."

A witty intellectual with meager expenses sells his books and, writing to his father, says: "Rejoice with me, father, for I'm finally supporting myself with my books."

CII. scholasticō aliquis dīcit: "Gāiī, in diē Martis hīc tē in somniīs vīsī." et ille: "mentīris!" dīcit, "nam in agrō eram."

To an intellectual someone said: "Gaius, on Tuesday I saw you here in my dreams." And he said: "You lie, for I was in the field."

CXXXVI. scholasticus Sīdōnius magistrem rogāvit: "quantum amphora quīnque congiōrum capit?" et ille dīxit: "loquerisne dē vīnō an oleō?"

A Sidonian scholar asked his teacher: "How much does a five-gallon jar hold?" and he said: "Are you talking about wine or oil?"

CXLVIII. lepidus ā tōnsōre garrulō: "quōmodo tē tondeam?" rogātus "tacitē," respondet.

A clever man, asked by the gossipy barber: "How shall I shave you?" replied: "Silently."

CLIII. lepidus luctāns in lutum cecidit atque, nē imperītus esse videātur, sē circumvertit et lutōsus per corpus tōtum glōriāns surrēxit.

A clever man who was wrestling fell into the mud and, so that he wouldn't seem to be unskilled, turned himself around and, muddy over his whole body, rose up gloating.

CCXV. domnaedius invidus vidēns inquilīnōs esse fēlīcēs, ex domō suā expulit.

A jealous landlord, seeing that his tenants were happy, kicked them out of his house.

CCXXXIV. ozostomos uxōrem rogāvit: "cāra, cūr mē ōdistī?" atque illa respondit: "quod tū mē bāsiās."

A man suffering from bad breath asked his wife: "Dear, why do you hate me?" And she replied: "Because you kiss me."

CCLV. scholasticus fīliō sepultō, magistrō eius occurrēns dīxit: "adīvitne fīlius?" respondit: "minimē." scholasticus dīxit: "deinde igitur, magister, mortuus est."

An intellectual, after his son had been buried, running into his son's teacher said to him: "Has my son been here?" The teacher replied: "No." The intellectual said: "Well anyway, he died."

CCLVI. scholasticus lūdīmagister audiēns discipulum esse aegrum, diē sequente eum esse febrīculōsum, secundō diē audiēns per eius patrem eum esse mortuum, dīcit: "sīc excūsandō nōn permittis līberōs discere."

An intellectual gym teacher, hearing that his student is unwell, the next day that he is feverish; the next day, hearing through the boy's father that he is dead, he says: "By making excuses thusly, you don't allow your children to learn."

IX

KINGS OF LATIN COMEDY

My Latin studies were focused on the epic mythologies of Vergil and Ovid, the historical and military accounts of Caesar and Livy, the love poetry of Catullus, and the orations of Cicero. A picture forms of a very serious and carefully cultivated society. But there are less serious and more raucous examples of Latin literature. The authors in this chapter are presented as a way to show this somewhat lighter (though at times darker) side of Latin literature. I hope that the reader will use this chapter as a starting point to explore comedic and satirical Latin works, for there are many other Latin jokesters for you to find.

PLAUTUS (CA. 254–184 BCE)

Plautus was a playwright who wrote a ton of plays. We know of about 130 different plays, but unfortunately only 20 have survived intact over the years. His works are the earliest complete Latin texts known to us. Plautus was a man of the people. Instead of writing in a super uptight style, he wrote in the more common style of the streets.

Many of Plautus's plays were translations or adaptations of Greek plays into both the Latin language and Roman situations. A lot of his work was also influenced by a Greek playwright whose name might come up in your history books: Meander. He is best known for the genre called Greek New Comedy.

Old Comedy was topical satire, which included references to current social situations and open mocking of public figures. Aristophanes is typically associated with Old Comedy. New Comedy was more like modern sitcoms, exploring how common stock characters would react to novel situations.

One of the new stock characters that Plautus introduced was the braggart soldier in his play *Miles Gloriosus*. When we meet the soldier, Pyrgopolinices, he is going over the records of his overblown accomplishments (including taking on an elephant) with his friend Artotrogus (who plays the role of the hapless hanger-on). After discussing how many enemies he has dispatched, they discuss one of Pyrgy's biggest problems: girls.

Art: amant tē omnēs mulierēs, neque iniūria,	Art: All women love you, and it's no injury,

quī sīs tam pulcher; vel illae quae here palliō	you who are so pretty; or there were those girls
mē reprehendērunt.	who grabbed me by the cloak yesterday . . .
Pyrg: quid eae dīxērunt tibi?	Pyrg: What did they say to you?
Art: rogitābant: "hīcine Achillēs est?" inquit mihi.	Art: They were asking: "Is he Achilles?" one says to me.
"immō eius frāter" inqūam "est." ibi illārum altera	"No, he is his brother," I say. Then the other of them
"ergō mecastor pulcher est" inquit mihi	says to me "therefore by Castor he is pretty
"et līberālis. vidē caesariēs quam decet.	And generous. See how comely his hair is.
nē illae sunt fortūnātae quae cum istō cubant."	Truly they are lucky who sleep with him."
Pyrg: itane aibant tandem?	Pyrg: They were really speaking like that?
Art: quaen mē ambae obsecrāverint,	Art. The girls who were both beseeching me
ut tē hodiē quasi pompam illa praeterdūcerem?	To take you past them like a parade?
Pyrg: nimiast miseria nimis pulchrum esse hominem.	Pyrg: It is too much misery to be such a pretty man.
Art: immō itast.	Art: Yes, indeed, it is.

Other stock characters that Plautus played with in his plays and helped cement into our collective unconscious were the *avārus* (the miser), *iuvenis amāns* (the young man in love), *servus callidus* (the clever slave), *servus stultus* (the stupid slave), *meretrīx* (the prostitute), and *lēnō* (the pimp).

CATULLUS (CA. 84–54 BCE)

Catullus was a poet who lived (and died) during the time of Julius Caesar. He was part of a poetic movement called the *poētae novī* (new poets), or "neoterics," by Cicero. The neoterics were the hipsters of ancient Rome: shirking the epic for a more personalized style; employing eclectic, old Greek meters; and fondly making obscure geographical and mythological references.

He is known especially for his love poetry, written to a mysterious woman he calls "Lesbia" (this is a reference to the Greek poet Sappho, who lived on the island Lesbos). The poems take place during different stages of the relationship: in one, Catullus is longing for her but is scared to speak; in another, he tells her he wants as many kisses from her as there are grains of sand. In the end, he longs for the time she used to love him. One of Catullus's best-known and shortest poems (85) sums up the uncertainty of his relationship (and perhaps, of all of them):

ōdī et amō, quārē id faciam, fortasse requīris?	I hate and love, why do I do it, perhaps you want to know?
nesciō sed fierī sentiō et excrucior	I don't know but I sense it happening and am tortured.

Catullus is also known for his invective, or insult, poetry. He playfully used these poems as weapons. In one poem (42), he summons all of his hendecasyllabics to help track down and reprimand a woman who has taken his writing tablets, and he threatens people with poetry in several other poems.

The invective poetry of Catullus and Martial is reminiscent in tone and content to rap battles. For example, he described the work of one of his rivals as *cacāta carta* (paper that has been defecated). He also writes to a man named Rufus who he says can't get girls because:

valle sub ālārum trux habitāre caper.	A mountain goat lives under his armpit.

But thankfully Catullus is there with a solution:

quārē aut crūdēlem nāsōrum interficere pestem	Therefore either kill the cruel scourge of noses
aut admīrārī dēsine cūr fugiunt	or stop wondering why the girls flee.

In poem 39, he praises Egnatius for his white smile. But this is a backhanded compliment. Catullus says that it wouldn't be an issue if he were from a city, but Egnatius is a Celtiber, hailing from Celtiberia in Middle Spain, so called because its people were thought to have been produced by a mixture of the Celts and the native Spaniards. Catullus says that it is custom in Celtiberia to follow a pretty gross teeth-cleaning regimen:

quod quisque mīnxit, hoc sibi solet māne	That which each urinated, it was customary for them in the morning

dentem atque russam dēfricāre gingīvam,	to brush their tooth and red gums,
ut quō iste vester expolītior dēns est,	so that with it that tooth of theirs is cleaner,
hoc tē amplius bibisse praedicet lōtī.	Further that this it is said that [he] has drunk this concoction.

One poem is written in response to two men who accused Catullus's poetry (and the poet) of being too sensitive and shameless. The poem (16) is not printed here in its entirety, because it contains very explicit content; so explicit that translators either came up with clever substitutions for the scurrilous words or did not translate them into English at all. Two (harmless) lines of the poem (16.5-6) must be shared because they sum up Catullus's philosophy of poetry and offer a good lens through which to read his work:

nam castum esse decet pium poētam	For it is fitting that a pious poet be moral
ipsum, versiculōs nihil necessest.	Himself, there is no necessity that his verses be [moral].

This is sentiment might well resonate in modern rap music. The full version of poem 16 is readily available online and is definitely NSFW. Read at your own risk.

Sadly, Catullus died when he was only 30 (unlike Cicero, who lived to be 63, and Augustus, who lived to be 76). The 116 poems he left us are thought to have been his only published works.

HORACE (65–8 BCE)

Horace was a part of the Golden Age of Latin poetry and the Augustan circle. His patron was Maecenas. He wrote a lot of formal poetry, experimenting with many different poetical forms and meters and exploring all sorts of different themes. His two books of *sermones* (conversations) are often called "the satires" in English. Most of his 18 dactylic hexameter poems are trying to illustrate a philosophical point. Horace's poems are infused with Epicureanism, the idea that the pleasures in life are to be enjoyed (in moderation).

One of Horace's most famous phrases, *carpe diem* (seize the day), is a perfect exposition of Epicurean philosophy. Lest you should think Horace's satires are devoid of humor, Epicurean philosophy is sprinkled throughout each poem, effectively illustrating the silly way some Romans chose to live in contrast to the ideals Horace offers.

The ninth poem, commonly called in English "The Boor," offers a classic comedic setup. I think of it as a scene from *Curb Your Enthusiasm*, with Horace playing Larry David:

ībam forte Viā Sacrā, sīcut meus est mōs	I was going by chance on the sacred way, just as is my custom
nescīō quid meditāns nūgārum, tōtus in illīs	thinking about I don't know what trifles, wholly in them.
accurrit quīdam nōtus mihi nōmine tantum	A certain man known to me by name only ran up
arreptāque manū, "quid agis, dulcissimē rērum?"	and having taken my hand said, "What's up, sweetest of things?"

Horace tries to shake the man and offers up excuses, but nothing works. The man wants to talk to Horace about his patron, Maecenas, and is eager to try to figure a way to break into the circle of accomplished poets. The man also happens to be needed in court on this day, and he asks Horace to come stand as a witness for him. Of course, Horace does not want to, but can't find a polite way to refuse, so he says okay. Somewhere along they way, they see someone who Horace thinks might be able to help him escape the guy:

Fuscus Aristius occurrit, mihi cārus et illum

Fuscus Aristius ran into us, dear to me and

quī pulchrē nōsset. cōnsistimus. "unde venīs et

someone who knew that guy very well. We stop: "From where are you coming and

quō tendis?" rogat et respondet. vellere coepī

where are you headed?" he asks and answers. I began to pull

et pressāre manū lentissima bracchia, nūtāns,

and press his arm very lightly with my hand, nodding,

distorquēns oculōs, ut mē ēriperet. male salsus,

distorting my eyes, so that he would snatch me away. He, badly witty,

rīdēns dissimulāre; meum iecur ūrere bīlīs.

Laughing, pretended to not notice; my liver burned with bile.

Eventually, Fuscus manages to get away, to Horace's dismay. But just when he thinks that he's going to be stuck with this guy all day, he's saved:

cāsū vēnit obvius illī	By chance came to meet him,
adversārius, et "quō tū, turpissime?" magnā	his accuser, and "where you going, most shameful one?"
inclāmat vōce et "licet antestārī?" ego vērō	he shouted with a great voice, and "can you stand witness?"
oppōnō auriculam. rapit in iūs; clāmor utrimque,	I truly offer my ear. He seizes him into the courtroom; an uproar on both sides,
undique concursus. sīc mē servāvit Apollō.	everywhere a crowd. Thus Apollo saved me.

At this point, I imagine Horace just disappearing into the crowd and going on his way to whatever else he was doing before this encounter (perhaps whistling nonchalantly with his hands in his toga pockets?).

TERENCE
(CA. 186/185–CA. 159 BCE)

Terence, a freed slave of Carthaginian (North African) descent, wrote six comedies that were, like Plautus's comedies, modeled on Greek originals. Because he lived a hundred of years after Plautus and was sold into a grammatically highbrow family of Latin speakers and writers, Terence's Latin is thought to be more approachable to introductory students than that of Plautus. It's said that he had other plays that were lost with him when he died at sea.

The selections below were not written by Terence but by a certain first-century scribe named Appolonaris, who added suitable prologues to each of Terence's plays. Terence had not actually included the standard prologue that describes the plot of the play to the audience; instead he used the time to defend his artistic choices to the audience. The following synopsis will not give you so much a flavor of Terence's Latin as the story lines of his play.

ADELPHOE	THE BROTHERS
duōs cum habēret Dēmea adulēscentulōs,	When Demea had two sons,
dat Miciōnī frātrī adoptandum Aeschinum,	He gave Aeschinus to his brother Micion to be adopted,
sed Ctesiphōnem retinet. hunc citharistriae	but kept Ctesipho. This one, captured
lepōre captum sub dūrō ac trīstī patre	by the charm of a cithara player, under a harsh and sad father
frāter cēlābat Aeschīnus; fāmam reī,	the brother Aeschinus was hiding; he was transferring,
amōrem in sēsē trānsferēbat; dēnique	love onto himself and the bad reputation for the thing; at last
fidicinam lēnōnī ēripit. Vitiāverat	he steals the cithara player from her pimp. Also
īdem Aeschīnus cīuem Atticam pauperculam	Aeschinus had corrupted a poor Athenian girl
fidemque dederat hanc sibi uxōrem fore.	And had given her his word that she would be his wife.
Dēmeā iūrgāre, grauiter ferre; mox tamen,	Demea scolds him and takes it badly, soon however,

| ut uēritās patefacta est, dūcit Aeschīnus | when the truth has been revealed, Aeschinus leads into marriage |
| uitiātam, potītur Ctesiphō citharistriam. | the girl he corrupted, Ctesipho gets the cithara player. |

PETRONIUS (CA. 27–66 CE)

Petronius has the distinction of having written one of the oldest European novels. His *Satyricon,* which survives only in large fragments, was an epic work of prose. The text follows the various exploits of a man named Encolpius and his young slave boy/lover, Giton. By following these two characters, we see into various facets of daily Roman life and get a taste of what life was like for normal(ish) people.

One of the most popular parts of the *Satyricon,* known as the "Cēna Trimālchiōnis," details a lavish Roman dinner party held by an ostentatious freedman named Trimalchio. Trimalchio seems to be trying too hard to overcome his past poverty. Interestingly, the original title for the novel *The Great Gatsby* was *Trimalchio in East Egg.* The character of Trimalchio and the setting of this ancient novel were sources of inspiration for F. Scott Fitzgerald when he wrote his novel, one of my favorites.

Our heroes are invited to dinner by a philosopher they know named Agamemnon. Agamemnon's slave describes their host like this:

"quid? vōs," inquit, "nescītis hodiē apud quem fīat? Trimalchiō, lautissimus homō. hōrologium in trīclīniō et būcinātōrem habet subōrnātum, ut subinde sciat quantum dē vītā perdiderit!"

The slave said: "What? You don't know whose house the party will be today? Trimalchio is a most luxurious man. He has a clock in his dining room and a decked-out trumpeter so that he can continually know how much from his life he has lost!"

Eager to get ready for the big dinner, Encolpius and Giton head for the bathhouse, where they happen to catch their first glimpse of their host for the night.

vidēmus senem calvum, tunicā vestītum russeā, inter puerōs capillātōs lūdentem pilā. Nec tam puerī nōs, quamquam erat operae pretium, ad spectāculum dūxerant, quam ipse pater familiae, quī soleātus pilā prasinā exercēbātur. Nec amplius eam repetēbat quae terram contigerat, sed follem plēnum habēbat servus sufficiēbatque lūdentibus.

We see a bald old man dressed in a ruddy tunic, playing with a ball among some long-haired boys. Not so much did the boys draw us to watch, although there was a reward of attention [to them], than did the father of the family himself, who, wearing sandals, was exercising with a green ball. Nor did he seek again further one that had touched the ground, but the slave had a full ball-bag and was supplying the players.

His next action seems to illustrate Trimalchio's character nicely:

Trimalchiō digitōs concrepuit, ad quod signum matellam spadō lūdentī subiēcit. Exonerātā ille vēsīcā aquam poposcit ad manūs, digitōsque paululum adspersōs in capite puerī tersit.

Trimalchio snapped his fingers, at which sign the eunuch put the chamber pot in front of him while he was playing. He, with his bladder unburdened, demanded water for his hands and wiped off his fingers, which were a little soaked, on the head of one of the boys.

They watch Trimalchio proceed through the rest of the bathhouse and then leave on a litter carried by four slaves, accompanied by a pipe-player. Our heroes follow and come to the house where they are greeted by well-dressed attendants (and a magpie), see a wall painting detailing Trimalchio's life, and are admitted to the feast. Eventually, Trimalchio is brought in on a litter, wearing fine clothes and too much bling. Then follows an elaborate Zodiac-themed meal with a dish for each astrological sign. After eating his fill, Encolpius gets the dirt on Trimalchio from the people sitting around him. The woman he has seen flitting about is Fortunata, Trimalchio's wife:

quem amat, amat; quem nōn amat, nōn amat.

Whom she likes, she likes; whom she doesn't like, she doesn't like.

Encolpius also learns all about Trimalchio's various friends, freedmen, and hangers-on. Trimalchio makes a long toast that everyone applauds and then even more food is brought out: boar, complete with birds that fly out when the boar is cut open. Like most dinner parties, soon they are talking about art and philosophy, and all manner of topics are addressed between several more courses of the meal.

JUVENAL
(CA. 55–CA. 127 CE)

Juvenal's 12 *Satires* give us an interesting view of some Roman customs and a mirror to hold up to our own society. Juvenal writes about what he sees as some of Rome's biggest social problems—hypocrisy, greed, and pedigree—and in support of compassion, knowledge of self, and moderation. Throughout his poems, he takes on (and showcases) aspects of Roman social life such as the patron-client relationship, government corruption, and poor patronage of the arts, and gives us a unique view into the world of first-century Rome.

Juvenal also writes from the point of view of (and for an audience consisting of) conservative upper-class Romans who felt threatened by what they perceived as a degradation of their society by foreigners and the lower classes. He has given us three of the most well known Latin phrases:

PĀNEM ET CIRCĒNSĒS
(BREAD AND CIRCUSES)

The phrase *pānem et circēnsēs*, often encountered when you study Roman history, refers to the practice of pacifying the Roman masses with free bread and free entertainment. There were frequent public holidays on which politicians and wealthy citizens staged theater or gladiatorial shows. *pānem et circēnsēs* comes from a passage in which Juvenal was commenting on the Roman mob, which made up most of the population of Rome.

nam quī dabat ōlim	For [the mob] that long ago gave away
imperium, fascēs, legiōnēs, omnia, nunc sē	sovereignty, power, armies, everything, now
continet atque duās tantum rēs ānxius optat:	preserves itself and anxious, hopes for only two things:
pānem et circēnsēs. "peritūrōs audiō multōs."	Bread and circuses. "I hear many will die."
"nīl dubium, magna est fornācula."	"No doubt, the oven is big."

MĒNS SĀNA IN CORPORE SĀNŌ (A HEALTHY MIND IN A HEALTHY BODY)

Two popular Latin phrases come from Juvenal's 10th satire. The phrase *mēns sāna in corpore sānō* is encountered in athletics and various educational contexts as an inspirational goal. The name of the shoe company ASICS is an acronym of the similar phrase *anima sāna in corpore sānō*. *mēns sāna in corpore sānō* comes at the end of the satire, after a long list of things that we desire but that will hurt us.

ōrandum est ut sit mēns sāna in corpore sānō,	You should pray for a healthy mind in a healthy body,
fortem posce animum mortis terrōre cārentem,	demand a strong spirit free of the fear of death,
quī spatium uītae extrēmum inter mūnera pōnat,	which places a long duration of life among the gifts of nature,
nātūrae, quī ferre queat quōscumque labōrēs,	which can bear whatever labors come,
nesciat īrāscī, cupiat nihil . . .	that does not know how to be angry, that desires nothing . . .
mōnstrō quod ipse tibi possīs	I show that which you yourself are able to give to yourself;
tranquillae per uirtūtem patet ūnica uītae.	the only seeds of tranquility certainly lie through virtue of life.
nūllum nūmen habēs, sī sit prūdentia: nōs tē,	You would have no divine power, if there were prudence:

nōs facimus, Fortūna, deam	We make you a goddess,
caelōque locāmus.	Fortune, and put you in the sky.

QUIS CUSTŌDIET IPSŌS CUSTŌDĒS (WHO WILL GUARD THE GUARDS THEMSELVES)

I have often encountered the phrase *quis custōdiet ipsōs custōdēs* (who will guard the guards themselves) in relation to politics and government, but it comes from Juvenal's sixth satire, which is about the perils of a very insecure man trying to keep his wife from falling in love with someone else and leaving him.

audiō quid veterēs ōlim moneātis amīcī,	I hear what you old friends once advised,
"pōne seram, cohibē." sed quis cūstōdiet ipsōs	"put up a bar, restrain her." But who will guard
custōdēs? cauta est et ab illīs incipit uxor.	those guards? She is cautious and begins with them.

MARTIAL (CA. 40–103 CE)

Martial was an invective poet who wrote during the time of three emperors, Domitian (r. 81-96 CE), Nerva (r. 96-98 CE), and Trajan (r. 98–117 CE) He was a master of epigrams, short poems that pack a punch. He is often described as an insult comic, and I would compare him to modern comics such as Mitch Hedberg or Jeff Ross. Some rap battles also involve this quick-witted invective turn of phrase. There is even an event I have seen at the O. Henry Pun-Off in Austin, Texas, in which poets exchange punny barbs.

In contrast to the small amount of poems we have from Catullus (116) and Juvenal (12), Martial's 12 books of epigrams contain over 1,500 poems and give us great insight into the political and social issues of his time (as well as great examples of wicked Latin burns). His poems are written primarily in elegiac couplets (see page 59 on meter).

In poem 1.16, Martial sums up his book of poems (and maybe this book, as well):

sunt bona, sunt quaedam mediocria, sunt mala plūra	There are good, there are some mediocre, there are many bad things
quae lēgis hic: aliter nōn fit, Auīte, liber.	which you read here: a book is not made otherwise, Auitus.

1.20 is a great play on the ambiguous phrase *sua carmina* ("his poems"):

carmina Paulus emit, recitat sua carmina Paulus.	Paul buys songs, Paul recites his songs.
nam quod emās possīs iūre uocāre tuum.	For what you buy you are able to legally call yours.

I.32, one of the first poems of Martial I can remember reading, is rather tame but very straightforward:

nōn amō tē, Sabidī, nec possum dīcere quārē:	I don't like you, Sabidius, and I'm not able to say why:
hoc tantum possum dīcere, nōn amō tē.	I am only able to say this, I don't like you.

1.47 is a good example of Martial's turns of phrase:

nūper erat medicus, nunc est vespillō Diaulus:	Recently he was a doctor, now he is an undertaker, Diaulus is:
quod vespillō facit, fēcerat et medicus.	what he does as an undertaker he also did as a doctor.

5.81 is an example of Martial's social commentary:

semper pauper eris, sī pauper es, Aemiliānē:	You will always be poor, if you are poor, Aemilianus:
dantur opēs nūllīs nunc nisi dīuitibus.	Riches are given to no one now except to the rich.

But most of Martial's poems are straight-up personal attacks. 12.20 is an excellent invective verse, accusing a rival of a dark problem:

quārē nōn habeat, Fabulle, quaeris	You ask, Fabullus, why Themison
uxōrem themisōn? habet sorōrem.	doesn't have a wife? he has a sister.

Many of Martial's poems take a tone that is this twisted, if not more extreme. But Martial also has a sensitive side, which he displays in a few love poems. In 12.46 he plays the tortured lover, which is reminiscent of Catullus 85 (above):

difficilis facilis, iūcundus acerbus es īdem:	Difficult and easy, pleasing and bitter you are at once:
nec tēcum possum vīvere, nec sine tē.	Neither with you am I able to live, nor without you.

Some of the poems are ambiguous. 5.82 could easily be read from the point of view of a jilted lover or a jilted client:

quid prōmittēbās mihi mīlia, Gaure, ducenta,	Why were you promising me 200,000, Gaurus,
sī dare nōn poterās mīlia, Gaure, decem?	If you were not able to give 10,000, Gaurus?
an potes et nōn uīs? Rogō, nōn est turpius istud?	Or are you able and you don't want to? I ask: is that not uglier?
ī, tibi dispereās, Gaure: pusillus homō es.	Go, you are undoing yourself, Gaurus: you are an insignificant person.

APULEIUS (124–170 CE)

Apuleius was born in Madurous, Numidia (modern-day Algeria), and lived in Carthage, the capital of the former Carthaginian empire, which had fallen under Roman rule. He attended school in Athens and lived under Roman rule. His writing is influenced by the language, stories, and philosophies of these cultures. Apuleius was a philosopher and prolific writer, well known in his day. Now he is more famous for his *Metamorphoses*, or *The Golden Ass*. It is the story of a man who dabbles in magic and accidently turns himself into a donkey. For the rest of the book, the man-donkey Lucius experiences the life of a slave to various owners and travels to different parts of the empire before he is turned back into a human and becomes a devotee of the goddess Isis (not to be confused with the modern terrorist organization).

A less well known collection of parts of his speeches, the *Florida*, contains myths, proverbs, and various tidbits from the writer's world. I found selection 13 particularly interesting: a description of parrots (*Indiae avis*, a bird of India) in which Apuleius talks about the method used to teach parrots how to speak (a similar technique also used to be used to teach Latin to human children):

ferreā clāviculā caput tunditur, imperium magistrī ut persentīscat.

Its head is beaten with an iron bar, so that it will perceive clearly the power of the teacher.

Apuleius tells us that parrots are best taught when they're young:

dum facile os, ut cōnfōrmētur, dum tenera lingua, utī convibrētur: senex autem captus et indocilis est et oblīviōsus.

While its mouth is limber, so that it can be formed, while its tongue is soft, so that it can be trilled: as an old parrot, however, it is lame and unteachable . . . and forgetful.

He says that the five-fingered parrots are the best kind of parrots, because their tongues are better equipped for the task:

id vērō, quod didicit, ita similiter nōbīs canit vel potius ēloquitur, ut, vōcem sī audiās, hominem putēs . . .

Truly that which it says, so similarly to us does it sing it [or rather speaks], if you were to hear its voice, you would think it was a human . . .

Ultimately, the parrot's vocabulary is based on that of its master:

et corvus et psittacus nihil aliud quam quod didicērunt prōnūntiant.
Both the crow and the parrot speak nothing other than what they learn.

sī convīcia docueris, convīciābitur diēbus ac noctibus perstrepēns maledictīs: hoc illī carmen est, hanc putat cantiōnem.
If you teach it taunts, it will taunt day and night, resounding with bad words: this to it is a tune, it thinks this is a song.

ubi omnia quae didicit maledicta percēnsuit, dēnuō repetit eandem cantilēnam.
When it has reviewed all the bad words it has learned, it repeats anew the same song.

sī carēre convīciō velīs, linguā excidenda est aut quam prīmum in silvās suās remittendus est.
If you should want to be free from its cry, you must cut out its tongue or you must set it free as soon as possible into its own woods.

X

HOW TO ROAST SOMEONE IN LATIN

One of the most common requests Latin students make is to learn how to curse at and insult their friends (and parents!). Although I generally like to follow the interests of the students, this is one area that I generally do not indulge, especially since across the country, our school system is currently trying to address the problem of bullying in schools. That's why I feel that a roast is the perfect context to introduce playful insults.

If you've ever seen a roast, you know that, in addition to the jokes and sometimes horrible things that are said about the people in attendance, at the end the participants praise those they've just roasted. The Friars Club claims on its website to have created the celebrity "roast" over a century ago. The club's motto is, "We only roast the ones we love." A Latin translation of this could be "tantum quōs amāmus torrēmus." This motto reflects the spirit in which the following section is presented.

Use the Latin in this section to host a roast for the Latinist in your life. And remember that anyone who is attending the roast is fair game, so spread the love around. Be prepared to take some barbs yourself; if not from the other guests, then from the person of honor, who traditionally gets to roast everyone else in the end. I have coined a new Latin proverb to address this reality of the roast:

sī aliōs torrēre vīs, parā torrērī ipse.	If you want to roast others, prepare to be roasted yourself.

Don't use the Latin in this section for evil. If you do, you may be regarded as a bad person, and I firmly believe that the evil you put out in Latin will come back to you (whether in Latin or not).

A lot of what makes a good roast performance is what makes a good joke performance. The main difference is the context: you are directly addressing the person you're making a joke about (or addressing audience members while they sit by, hopefully not glaring too hard). If you're interested in roasting someone in Latin, you're best to combine the various elements and use them as the context calls for them (as illustrated below). The invective material especially may come in handy.

ROASTING

The general term for roast I will be using is *torrēre*, because the term for a roast was not used as the name of an event. We can use the somewhat roundabout phrase *cēna torrendō* (literally, a dinner for roasting). One of the more popular phrases with the kids these days is "burn." Here is how to say it in Latin with some examples:

ambūrere	to burn
ō! tē bene ambussit!	Oh! They burned you good!
ambustio	burn
vīsne glaciem cum ambustiōne illā?	Do you want ice with that burn?
ambustus/ambusta	burned/scorched
tū ambustus es!	You got burned!
ambustionem aegram!	sick burn!
ambustionem!	burn!

CALLING SOMEONE OUT

If the person being roasted is present . . .

___ videō in spectātōribus. ___ adest; grātiās prō veniendō!
I see ___ in the audience. ___ is here; thanks for coming!

And if he or she is not present . . .

___ nōn videō. ___ abest. mīror cūr nōn adsit. fortassē vōs nōn amat.
I don't see ___. ___ is absent. I wonder why they're not here. Maybe they don't like you all.

BASIC INSULTS

___ es.	quam ___ es!	tam ___ es!
You are ___.	How ___ you are!	You are so ___!

absurdus	silly, out of tune, incongruous
āmens	foolish, out of one's mind
bardus	dull, stupid
brūtus	brute, dumb, oaf
incallidus	unskillful, simple
infacētus	coarse, rude, blunt
insciens	ignorant, unknowing
inscītus	ignorant, inexperienced
stultus	stupid, foolish
pusillus	very small, insignificant

GRAMMATICA

All of the above are adjectives and must agree
in gender (type) with the noun they modify. For
adjectives like *absurdus,* you change the *-us* to *-a*
when referring to feminine. *āmens* would be the
same for masculine or feminine nouns.

NAMES TO CALL

asinus	donkey, ass
blennus	simpleton
caudex	blockhead (tree trunk)
fungus	dolt, mushroom
gurdus	numbskull
truncus	blockhead (tree trunk)

GRAMMATICA

The case called the "vocative" is used when directly addressing someone or something. It makes its appearance only in words that end in -us. If you are talking about someone and saying that he or she is a donkey, you would say "___ est asinum." If you are directly addressing the donkey in question, say "asine!" As in asine! abī! (You ass! Go away!).

MORE COMPLEX INSULTS

vidēris esse . . .	You look like . . .
canis	a dog
xylospongium	a sponge on a stick (used to clean oneself in the public Roman toilets)
___ ōdī plūs quam lūnō Aenēan ōdit.	I hate ___ more than Juno hates Aeneas.

___ ōdī plūs quam Hannibal Rōmam ōderit.	I hate ___ more than Hannibal hated Rome.

The Greek philosopher Socrates had a reputation for being very ugly, so he's a good metric to use in jokes targeting someone's looks:

Sōcratēs est tam foedus ut Medūsam in saxum mūtāret.	Socrates is so ugly that he would turn Medusa into stone.
tam foedus es, prope tē Sōcratēs est pulcherrimus hominum!	You are so ugly, next to you Socrates is the prettiest of all men!
cūr Sōcratēs nihil sciat, fortassē requīris?	Why does Socrates know nothing, maybe you ask?
tam foedus est ut Vēritās eum fūgit.	He is so ugly that the Truth flees from him.

PRAISING

The word *laudāre* means "to praise." *honōrāre* means "to honor."

LAUS PRAISE, COMMENDATION

tē laudō.	I praise you.
tē honōrō.	I honor you.
tibi laudem dō.	I give praise to you.

BASIC TERMS OF ENDEARMENT

amīcus friend

amīculus a dear friend, boyfriend

mel honey

oculus apple of my eye
(literally, just eye)

amīcula a dear friend, girlfriend

intimus a very intimate friend

dēlicia darling, sweetheart

columba dove

POSITIVE QUALITIES

meritus deserving, worthy

dulcissimus sweetest

piissimus most pious,
faithful, loyal

sanctissimus must sacred

rārissimus very rare

amantissimus most loving, kind

cārissimus dearest

pientissimus most dutiful,
godly

optimus best

incomparābilis unequaled

dignissimus most worthy,
deserving

bonus good

MORE COMPLEX COMPLIMENTS

____ amō/dīligō.

____ est homō mihi dīlectus.

____ est ūnus/ūna optimōrum
quōs cognōvī.

I love ____.

____ is my favorite person.

____ is one of the best people
I have ever met.

gaudeō me eum/eam cognōvisse.	I am glad that I met him/her.
hodiē ___ laudandus/a est.	Today, ___ must be praised.
tū vidēris formōsior quam rosā.	You look more beautiful than a rose.
tam callida es, prope tē Sōcratēs est stultissimus hominum!	You are so clever, next to you Socrates is the stupidest of men!

A CAUTIONARY TALE: CICERO'S LAST ROAST

Before we get to the (pretend) roast of Julius Caesar, it is important to note that the roast would not have gone over very well in Roman times. The roast is really a unique product of modern times.

It is useful to look at what happened to our old friend Cicero when he roasted Mark Antony in the Senate to gain some perspective on how special it is to live in a country where politicians are roasted live by comedians yearly at the White House Correspondents' Dinner, where political candidates roast each other at charity dinners, and where ordinary citizens can freely tweet nonsense at the president of the United States and he at them.

In the wake of Julius Caesar's assassination, Cicero delivered a series of speeches against Caesar's former head general, Mark Antony, whom he accused of being a tyrant. After Mark Antony and the future emperor Octavian had joined in an alliance, they started putting proscriptions (bounties) out for their various political enemies. Cicero ended up on one of these lists.

The story goes that Cicero was en route to a ship that would take him safely from the political turmoil in Rome when he was stopped by a soldier and the informant who had betrayed him. Cicero gave himself up and, according to the writer Seneca, said: "accēde veterāne, et sī hoc saltim potes rectē facere, incīde cervīcem" (approach veteran, and if you at least are able to do this correctly, cut my neck).

The soldier complied. Not only was Cicero beheaded, but his hands (or hand, depending on which writer you read) were also cut off and put on display in the Roman forum. Everyone would have understood the message being sent when they saw the dead orator's hands nailed to the rostrum, the platform in the forum provided for public speeches.

ROAST OF JULIUS CAESAR

gaudeō vōbīscum adesse ut Gāium Iūlium Caesarem honōrēmus, quod sī nōn eum honōrārēmus nūllī nunc essēmus vīvī.

I am glad to be here with you all to honor Gaius Julius Caesar, because if we weren't honoring him, none of us would be alive right now.

Caesarī faveō. eī crēdō. Caeser Rōmam iterum magnam fierī vult, tam magnam quam erat in diēbus reī pūblicī prīmīs, paucīs novīs additīs. quae sunt ipse scit. necesse est tibi eī crēdere, ut uxor ēius eī crēdit.

I support Caesar. I believe in him. Caesar wants to make Rome great, as great as it was in the first days of the republic, with just a few new things added on. He knows what those are. Just trust him. As his wife trusts him.

Caesar vidētur ut sī Pānos atque Vulcānī īnfans. nesciō quid tuī amōrem Cleopātrae cēpit: pecūnia an imperium? sānē non faciēs illa.

Caesar looks like the baby of Pan and Vulcan. I don't know what of yours captured Cleopatra's love: money or power? It certainly wasn't that face.

itinera multa fēcit et multās rēs transīvit: montēs, flūmina, Senātum.

He has made many trips and crossed over many: mountains, rivers, the Senate.

citō arcesse medicum aliquis! nōn certus sum an dē rīdendō quatit. fortassē est morbus ēius comitiālis?

Quickly, somebody send for a doctor! I'm not sure if he's shaking from laughing. Maybe it's his epilepsy?

Caesar quoque pessimus scriptōrum est. satis malum est tē tam multōs feminās līberōsque Gallōs innocentēs occīdisse, peior etiam mē scripta tua lēgisse!

Caesar is also the worst of writers; like, it's bad enough that you killed so many defenseless Gallic women and children, but what's worse was that I had to read what you wrote about it!

sed satis iocōrum. vērē Caesar est ūnus optimōrum. multās rēs bonās Rōmae fēcit atque fēcerit.

But that's enough of jokes. Truly, Caesar is one of the best. Many good things he has done and will have done for Rome.

omnēs! tollite pōcula! Caesar, tē moritūrum salūtāmus! sit vīta tibi sine cultrīs. avē, Caesar!

Everyone! Raise your cups! Caesar, you who are about to die we salute! May your life be without knives. Hail, Caesar!

APPENDIX

AUTHORS

Apuleius (124–170 CE): Philosopher and writer of *Metamorphoses*, also referred to as *The Golden Ass*.

Caesar (100–44 BCE): General, dictator, and writer of *De Bello Gallico* and *De Bello Civilo*.

Catullus (84–54 BCE): Poet, writer of whose work we have 114 poems, commonly referred to as the *Carmina*.

Cicero (106–43 BCE): Orator, consul, and writer, who wrote many philosophical and practical treatises. Many of his letters to friends and relatives also have survived.

Descartes (1596–1650 CE): French philosopher whose famous *Meditations on First Philosophy* were written in Latin.

Ennius (ca. 239–169 BCE): Poet sometimes referred to as the father of Latin poetry, who wrote with Greek poetic forms. Only fragments of his works survive.

Horace (65–8 BCE): Poet. Several books of his poetry have survived.

Juvenal (55 to 60–ca. 127 CE): Satirical poet. 16 of his satires have survived.

Manilius (1st century CE): Poet who wrote the *Astronomicon*, an epic poem about Roman astronomical beliefs.

Martial (ca. 40–ca. 103 CE): Comedic poet. 14 books of his epigrams have survived.

Livy (59 BCE–17 CE): Historian who wrote an epic history of Rome called *ab urbe condita* (from the founding).

Suetonius (ca. 69–122 CE): Biographer who wrote the *Lives of the 12 Caesars*, biographies of the first 12 Roman emperors.

Ovid (ca. 43 BCE–17 CE): Poet most famous for his mythological epic *Metamorphoses*. Many other of his works have survived.

Petronius (ca. 27–66 CE): Senator and writer who is thought to have written the *Satyricon*. No other works of his have survived.

Plautus (ca. 254–184 BCE): Playwrite who wrote comedies. 20 of his plays have survived.

Quntilian (ca. 35–100 CE): Teacher and writer, whose *Institutio Oratiora* reveals much about speaking and teaching the Latin language.

Seneca (ca. 4 BCE–65 CE): Philosopher who also wrote tragedies. Many of his letters have also survived.

Terence (ca. 186/185–ca. 159 BCE): Playwrite and former slave who wrote comedies. 6 of his plays have survived.

Vergil (70–19 BCE): Poet most famous for his epic poem *The Aeneid*. Other collections of shorter poems, the *Georgics* and the *Eclogues* have also survived. Sometimes his name is also spelled Virgil.

NUMBERS

Cardinal numbers tell how many of something there are. They answer the question *quot?* (how many?).

1 ūnus, ūna, ūnum	15 quīndecim	29 ūndētrīgintā
2 duo, duae	16 sēdecim	30 trīgintā
3 trēs, tria	17 septendecim	40 quadrāgintā
4 quattuor	18 duodēvīgintī	50 quīnquāgintā
5 quīnque	19 ūndēvīgintī	60 sexāgintā
6 sex	20 vīgintī	70 septuāgintā
7 septem	21 vīgintī ūnus	80 octōgintā
8 octō	22 vīgintī duo	90 nōnāgintā
9 novem	23 vīgintī trēs	100 centum
10 decem	24 vīgintī quattuor	
11 ūndecim	25 vīgintī quīnque	
12 duodecim	26 vīgintī sex	
13 tredecim	27 vīgintī septem	
14 quattuordecim	28 duodētrīgintā	

Ordinal numbers tell the order of something. They answer the question *quota?* (which one [in a series]?). They are adjectives and change their endings based on the noun they modify.

1st	prīmus	20th	vīcēsimus
2nd	duo, duae	21st	vīcēsimus prīmus
3rd	trēs, tria	22nd	vīcēsimus secundus
4th	quattuor	23rd	vīcēsimus tertius
5th	quīnque	24th	vīcēsimus quārtus
6th	sex	25th	vīcēsimus quīntus
7th	septem	26th	vīcēsimus sextus
8th	octō	27th	vīcēsimus septimus
9th	novem	28th	duodētrīcēsimā
10th	decem	29th	ūndētrīcēsimā
11th	ūndecimus	30th	trīcēsimā
12th	duodecimus	40th	quadrāgēsimus
13th	tertius decimus	50th	quīnquāgēsimus
14th	quārtus decimus	60th	sexāgēsimus
15th	quīntus decimus	70th	septuāgēsimus
16th	sextus decimus	80th	octōgēsimus
17th	septimus decimus	90th	nōnāgēsimus
18th	duodēvīcēsimus	100th	centēsimus
19th	ūndēvīcēsimus		

RECOMMENDATIONS FOR FURTHER EXPLORATION

LISTENING

One of the best things that you can do to help yourself learn to speak Latin is to immerse yourself in "input," spoken or written Latin. Several high-quality Latin podcasts have recently been released that provide an excellent source of listening practice. There are also several resources around the web where you can find Latin to listen to.

Quomodo Dicitur: Three friends, Gus Grissom, Jason Slanga, and Justin Slocum Bailey, conduct a weekly conversation in Latin. They discuss *quo libet* (whatever is pleasing). Topics have included health and wellness, letters by the philosopher Seneca, and Morgan Freeman! http://quomododicitur.com

Sermones Raedarii: Alessandro Conti records his podcast in the car during his commute in Verona. He talks about various topics related to Latin teaching and features "Fabulae Raedariae," a retelling of classic fairy tales that are perfect for listening practice. Sometimes he even has a passenger along for the ride! http://sermonesraedarii.wordpress.com

Indwelling Language's Latin Listening Project: The Latin Listening Project is a collection of videos of people talking about their lives in Latin. A large collection of short videos are currently on the site and potentially more are to come, as the site is crowd-sourcing its videos and has instructions on how you can participate.

There is a wide variety of Latin on the internet that you can listen to (and watch). The site also features "Limen: A Latin Teaching Portal," which can provide information and inspiration to aspiring and seasoned Latin teachers. The site is curated by Justin Slocum Bailey, of the Quomodo Dicitur podcast. http://indwellinglanguage.com/latin

Latinitium: Latinitium is Daniel Pettersson's online Latin hub, where there are podcasts to listen to, videos to watch, and articles to read on a variety of topics, from biographies of Latin authors to retellings of stories, some that are well known and some that you may have never heard. http://www.latinitium.com

YouTube: You can find a lot of videos in Latin or about Latin on YouTube. But be careful. You can also find a lot of raw, unfiltered student Latin projects there, though some are very well done. Many of those that are not quite so high quality are at least good for a laugh.

SAMOHI Latin Media: Two Latin films have been produced this century by Latin students at Santa Monica High School. The first production is called *Pacifica*, a highly watchable four-part high-school drama series in the vein of *The O.C.*. The trailer is on YouTube at https://youtu.be/SEMmbxAHycY. The second film is called *Barnabas and Bella*, a musical about a new student who falls for a popular girl. It is available online at https://vimeo.com/81824982.

READING

More than enough Latin is lying around on the Internet to keep a person happy for several lifetimes. Many of the works that are available online have not been translated into English, or if they have, it was a really long time ago.

The Latin Library: The Latin Library provides hours of reading material by the major authors of Latin literature. Latin from all historical eras is represented, from Classical Latin to Medieval Latin to Neo-Latin. Perfect for casual reading on the go. http://www.thelatinlibrary.com

Perseus Digital Library: The Perseus Digital Library is great for more in-depth analysis of Latin texts (I spent a lot of time in college on this site). The site has many Latin and Greek texts that are hyperlinked, cross-referenced, and annotated. A must-visit for scholars-in-training. http://www.perseus.tufts.edu

Novellas: A recent trend toward Latin-language novellas has produced engaging works that are highly comprehensible and written with a limited vocabulary, rich with a variety of grammatical contexts. I hope this trend continues, both as a Latin teacher and as a reader:

Brando Brown Canem Vult. An introductory-level story about a boy who wants a dog, originally written in Spanish by Carol Gabb, translated into Latin by Justin Slocum Bailey.

Cloelia. A reader by Ellie Arnold that sees Rome through the eyes of a woman.

Iter mirabile Dennis et Debrae. About a pair of time-traveling friends who go to ancient Rome and meet Julius Caesar, by Christopher Buczek.

Itinera Petri. An intermediate-level fantasy adventure by Bob Patrick.

Marcus et Imagines Suae Bonae. An introductory-level story about a boy who doesn't like school, originally written in Spanish by Magaly Rodriguez, translated by John Bracey and Lance Piantaggini.

Piso Ille Poetulus. A Latin poetry novel set in ancient Rome by Lance Piantaggini.

Pluto: fabula amoris. A retelling of the story of Pluto and Persephone by Rachel Ash and Miriam Patrick.

Google Books: Google has an unexpectedly large collection of free Latin books from throughout the ages, some several hundred years old (those are often printed in difficult-to-read typesets, though). These texts range from classic Latin authors to Latin primers from the 19th and 20th centuries. Some of the primers offer much better comprehensible input than do modern Latin textbooks.

Beginners' Latin by the Direct Method by Edward C. Chickering and Harwood Hoadley

Fabulae Facilaes by Frank Ritchie

Initium by Reginald Bainbridge Appleton and W. H. S. Jones

Ora Maritima by E. A. Sonnenschein

Pons Tironum by Reginald Bainbridge Appleton and W. H. S. Jones

Pro Patria by E. A. Sonnenschein

Puer Romanus by Reginald Bainbridge Appleton and W. H. S. Jones

The Shorter Latin Primer by Benjamin Hall Kennedy

Via Romana by Frank Stephen Granger

SPEAKING

Unless you really like talking to yourself in the mirror, you'll probably want to try out the Latin you're learning by interacting with other Latin speakers.

SALVI: The North American Institute of Living Latin Studies: This site has resources for beginning and advanced Latin speakers. SALVI also offers Latin immersion camps (Rusticatio) and weekend getaways (Biduum) across the country. The site has more information on how you can join the ever-growing community of Latin speakers. http://www.latin.org

Paideia Institute: This organization is dedicated to active classical language education. They host a Living Latin program in Rome and organize various Living Latin and Living Greek programs. http://www.paideiainstitute.org

Latin meetups: In addition to SALVI, many scattered, grassroots Latin groups gather either for in-person meetups for dinner or coffee or for online meetups that span oceans. You can find them by using Internet search tools and by hooking into groups of Latin speakers on Facebook and Twitter.

WRITING

The ability to write in Latin is the true untapped portion of the four language skills for the Latin-speaking community. Latin speakers can really let their creativity and personal vision shine when they write. A reading audience is definitely out there, however small, for whatever you would like to write in Latin.

Please note that most so-called composition texts don't actually teach you how to write in Latin. These texts are usually wonderful resources for learning the nuances of Latin and English grammar, because the primary goal is to translate English sentences into Latin, but this is not the same as composing. Always make it your goal when writing in Latin to produce a message that can be understood by another Latin speaker who will be reading it.

VOCABULARY

The following are the primary online dictionaries that I use and that I used during the preparation of this book:

William Whitaker's Words: This dictionary is wonderful for looking up basic word meanings and very helpful for its grammatical analysis. Type in any Latin word and it will tell you what the word means and all its possible grammatical explanations. http://archives.nd.edu/words.html

Numen: The Latin Lexicon: My go-to mobile Latin dictionary, this site is great for in-depth study of vocabulary terms both Latin-English and especially English-Latin. http://latinlexicon.org

ACKNOWLEDGMENTS

I would like to initially thank Melody McCormick, for she inspired me to study Latin in the 10th grade and guided me in the first few years of the journey on which I now find myself writing this book.

Thanks also to the staff at Bellaire High School in Houston, Texas; Powell Elementary School in Washington, DC; and Dripping Springs High School in Dripping Springs, Texas. These schools have given me the ability to develop and hone my teaching and Latin-speaking abilities.

Thanks to Casie Vogel and the team at Ulysses Press for giving me the opportunity to work on this project and working so well with me throughout the process. Thanks to Derek for your eagle eyes. Many thanks as well to Cammie Thomson, whose sharp eyes spotted this opportunity in the first place. Also to Johan Winge, creator of the Latin Macronizer (http://stp.lingfil.uu.se/~winge/macronizer), which was quite useful in the preparation of this text.

Above all, thank you to my many students who have, over the years, learned with me and also taught me so much.

ABOUT THE AUTHOR

Jason Talley is a musician and Latin teacher who uses engaging, interactive, and immersive techniques to share his love of Latin with his students. After graduating from the University of Texas with a BA in Latin, he has been a tutor and public school Latin teacher. Though he originally chose Latin because of its status as an unspoken, dead, language, he now enjoys instructing new learners to speak the language. Jason even uses his free time for Latin pursuits such as translating pop songs and writing Latin originals. He resides outside Austin in the beautiful Texas Hill Country with his wife and two children. You can follow his Latin Twitter account: @magistertalley.